Take My Hand

Written by Peter Lowsley

Published by Hero Publishing
Copyright © Peter Lowsley 2009

Cover design by Joanna Lowsley

Printed in England

ISBN 978-0-9562806-0-2

For Joseph Alan

A True Tale of the Unexpected

Far, far away in a place somewhere north of Watford, unbelievable events have started to unfold.

Those who live in the beautiful south will tell you that at the wilderness end of the M62 sits a forlorn and forgotten city. They'll say that this place used to be famous for having a thriving fishing industry. That part at least is true, until the rug was finally pulled from under hard working men and their families of course. These people will make further claims that this bleak wasteland is now infamous as the place which tops the leagues for all the wrong reasons.

Hull has always been an easy target but in recent years it has become almost fashionable to knock the place. People who know little or even less about Hull but who do have a keen eye for a headline and a strong nose for a fast buck have lined up to give us a kicking. We have featured both regularly and prominently in Dan Kieran's 'Crap Towns' books. The Duchess of York jumped onboard the gravy train by picking Hull as the place most in need of her touch, when she taught a local family how to eat properly. Kirsty and Phil from 'Location, Location,' reckon that Hull is the worst place to live in the entire universe. Even Trinny and Susannah got in on the act when they painted a pretty bleak picture of Hull a couple of years ago, based almost solely on the fact that we didn't have a top flight football team.

For the uneducated Hull has always been regarded as merely a Rugby League stronghold. In truth football has played just as much a part in the lives of the ordinary people of Hull as the oval ball game. My dad took me to Boothferry Park religiously when I was a kid. We'd catch the train from Paragon station and get off at the halt right alongside the ground. Standing on the terraces in all weathers, we watched Wagstaff, Chilton and a succession of City heroes ply their considerable trade. I'll always be thankful to my Dad for that black and amber legacy. Thanks also to promotion into the biggest and best football league in the world, with millions of followers across the globe; everyone is getting to know the name of Hull. This time let's just hope it is for the right reasons.

The Tigers would be competing in the English Premier League for the very first time this season. One thing was certain; holding our own amongst the big boys wasn't going to be easy. We would end up facing some of the best teams and many of the greatest players in the world. We would also have to fight the overwhelming weight of popular opinion but coming from Hull at least that would be something that we were used to.

I hope you like this book and I hope you end up enjoying the season. Most of all, as we start out on the journey I can't help thinking that we are all hoping for a happy ending to the tale.

Before I go any further, I'd like to say a special thank you to the following people for giving me the invaluable inspiration and encouragement to write this book.
I am confident that whenever this team crosses the white line they will step up to the plate and grab the shirt.

My team (four, four, two)

1 Joanna

2 Joe	5 Alice	6 Steve	3 Finn
7 Paul	4 Tony	8 Phil	11 Gary
	9 Dave	10 Milo	

The warm up

In 1971 my dad managed to get tickets for the FA Cup final. The biggest game I had seen up to then was the Watney Cup Semi Final almost a year earlier. Manchester United came to town that summer night with Charlton, Best and Law all in the line up. It was the first game in England to be settled on penalties, with Best being the first to score and Law being the first to miss. Our Goalkeeper Ian McKechnie became the first to take a penalty and then the first to miss one. It was a night of many firsts but sadly we ended up coming second.

As cup final day grew closer my excitement reached fever pitch. The game still burns brightly in my memory. I supported Liverpool on the day, only because it is nearer to Hull you understand. My dad told me that Arsenal would win 2-1, just to annoy me of course. I remember it was a very hot day. The game was goalless at the end of ninety minutes and extra time was needed. A year earlier the final between Leeds and Chelsea had gone to a replay, I hoped that this game wouldn't go the same way. We sat sweltering on wooden benches at one side of the pitch towards the tunnel end. In the first half of extra time Steve Heighway scored first for Liverpool from what looked to me like an impossible angle. Eddie Kelly equalised with a scruffy goal for the Gunners. In the second half of extra time Charlie George scored his memorable winner and fell backwards with his hands aloft in an even more memorable celebration. So Arsenal did win 2-1 in the end, my dad just smiled. As we walked away from the twin towers down Wembley Way I stuck close to my dad so that I didn't get swallowed up and lost in the huge, noisy, bustling crowd.

"Do you think City will ever play at Wembley?" I said.

He looked down at me and again he just smiled.

I've never been very keen on Andy Williams, with his sensible knitwear and music to watch the girls go by. I don't even think that he's a particularly good singer. I mean, just listen to the way he struggles to reach the high notes on even his most easy listening tunes. My mam used to accuse him of not singing anything particularly strenuous.

At first, his version of our unofficial anthem Take My Hand, seemed an odd choice to play after the final whistle at Wembley. We could have had any of the many versions of the song including the most famous one by the King himself. When I thought about it though, I realised that Andy Williams was a good choice. His version of the timeless classic moves along at a decent pace and everyone can take part with no fear of being out sung. At any rate I can't hear the song now without thinking about that glorious, sunny day in May. It was the day thousands of us hugged friends, family and total strangers and sang along with Andy Williams. It was the day Deano broke Bristol hearts with a wonder goal that I will never get tired of seeing. It was the day we were promoted to the top flight for the very first time. It was the day most of us thought we'd never see.

Like many others we had decided to make a weekend of it in London. We booked a family room in a nice little hotel near the South side of London Bridge. I woke up early on the day of the game, more excited than nervous. In fact I don't remember having any nerves at all. In the back of my mind I knew that Phil Brown's meticulous preparation would see us through, so why worry? My intention was to enjoy the weekend and leave the rest to Phil and his team. I decided to go for a run along the Thames, wearing my lucky City socks and listening to my lucky songs on my lucky ipod. Pounding the South Bank down towards Westminster, I saw the odd street cleaner and fellow runner as I took in the sights in the quiet, early part of the day. I crossed the bridge at Westminster and headed back along the

North Bank. Where the first leg had been in the shade and easy going, the return journey was very warm and a lot less pleasant, as the sun came out to hinder my progress. I struggled over London Bridge back to the hotel, with only my music for company. Joey Ramone's version of the Louis Armstrong classic 'What A Wonderful World,' came on to give me a lift. As I jogged the final few yards back to the hotel I think I knew then that it was going to be our day.

Unlike my run, both legs of the play off semi final against Watford had been relatively comfortable. Before that balmy evening at the KC stadium when we finally put Watford to the sword, we enjoyed a tenser but equally satisfying game at their place. Despite all their bravado and insistence that the tie was still alive, the majority of Watford fans must have realised that after going down 2-0 at home the game was all but up. As we walked away from Vicarage Road I overheard a young Watford fan talking to his mates.

"I bet they can't even afford a trip to Wembley anyway," he said. He was referring to us poor northerners of course. Well for the benefit of that particular hapless Hornet, I have to say that I sold my whippet and racing pigeons put the family on a strict, money saving diet of bread and dripping and managed to scrape enough brass together for the big day down in the capital. It was a ridiculously expensive weekend but to paraphrase the credit card advert, seeing your club play and win at Wembley and secure top flight status for the first time in their history was absolutely priceless.

On the return to Hull after Wembley, Phil Brown made a proclamation from the balcony of the City Hall in his broad north east accent.

"We won wor first trip to Wembley and we will survive wor first visit to the Premier League." Brave words, perhaps even alcohol fuelled words but along with our chairman Paul Duffen and the rest of the team, the desire to succeed was there for everyone to see.

An assumption was made by football luminaries that because we were promoted through the play offs we would be at least three weeks behind in our preparations. Well respected football personalities like Bobby Robson and Terry Venables tipped us to fail with typical percentage predictions. Their views were based on what had happened in the past to teams like Watford and Derby. In actual fact plans had been drafted weeks if not months earlier when it became clear that promotion was a very real possibility. As a result the club had been very detailed in preparation and extremely active in attracting good quality personnel. Despite a fairly mediocre finish to the pre season games, our manager and his team were satisfied that they had done everything in their power to prepare us for the big day, the start of the 2008/2009 Premier League campaign.

The Kick off

Hull City 2 Fulham 1
Saturday 16th August 2008

Before the fixtures came out we had hoped for a home game in the first match, anything more would be a bonus. While acutely aware that there would be no easy games in the Premier League, it was clear to us that some would be easier than others. Without being disrespectful, the first three games of Fulham, Blackburn and Wigan, should certainly give us our best chance of getting the kind of start we needed. At least that's how it looked on paper.

The opening day brought the added poignancy of Paul Duffen ringing the Premiership bell to mark our arrival in the top flight. He spoke very eloquently as he'd also done at Wembley, remembering the Tigers fans who hadn't lived to see this momentous occasion. It was an extra special day for us. Our seven year old Joe had been chosen to join Paul's seven year old twins as match mascots. I got a call from Alison from the club at the start of the season asking which game we wanted for Joe.

"I should warn you that the big games have gone," she said.

"Oh have they?"

"Yes, you can't have Manchester United, Liverpool, Chelsea or Arsenal."

"What about the opening match against Fulham?" I asked.

"That's still free; Joe can be the mascot for that game."

As far as I was concerned this was the most historic game in our history. Just imagine being the Hull City mascot at their first ever Premier League game, isn't that something to be able to tell people in years to come? I asked Joe's older brother Milo, if he would like to go with him on to the pitch. Milo is, to say the least, totally football barmy and probably Ian Ashbee's biggest fan. I knew that he would get far more out of the day than I would and maybe even more than Joe himself. He went on to describe the event as the best day of his life. The best way I can describe Milo is twenty four going on seven.

It was the number seven in the shape of Fulham striker Seol Ki-Hyeon who threatened to ruin our day. He took advantage of some poor defending to head home neatly from a precise Jimmy Bullard ball, around the seven minute mark. At this point I sat with my head in my hands thinking that perhaps we would be in for a thrashing, maybe seven, as Fulham continued to press forward with fast, slick Premier League style football. Gradually we became accustomed to the pace of the game and a solo wonder strike from Geovanni got us back on level terms. The combination of Brazilian skill and some lamentable finishing from Fulham's Zoltan Gera left the game finely poised.

"He couldn't hit a bull's arse with a banjo," I said, aiming my criticism at the hopeless Hungarian. The second half saw the introduction of our own marvellous Magyar, Peter Halmosi. We adopted a more attacking style of play and it was our turn to put Fulham on the rack. When Phil Brown brought on Fagan and Folan, their well worked supply and finish saw us hold the record that evening, as the only team that had won every Premier League game they had ever played.

The sun was shining and the fans were happy. No, that's not right, they were over the moon. Two seasons ago we were almost relegated from the Championship. We survived and then went on to win promotion to the Premier League. We did it by making our first ever trip to Wembley and winning the play off final. Not only that but local hero Dean Windass scored the goal that won us that game. The opening day of the season saw us take on and beat an established top flight team to get precisely the sort of start we'd all been crossing our fingers and hoping for. Who was writing this stuff, Hans Christian Anderson?

That night I tuned in to Match of the Day for the first time since I really can't remember when. City got headline coverage and we even had a glimpse of Joe proudly leading the team out. The unholy trinity of Lineker, Hansen and Shearer charted new territory as they gave positive assessments and generous comments in favour of the unfashionable new boys. I had to rub my eyes, was I was dreaming? I hoped not, I'd hate to step out of the shower like Bobby Ewing did in Dallas, only to find that we had actually been relegated the season before last and Leeds United had been the team that went on to the Premier League.

Blackburn Rovers 1 Hull City 1
Saturday 23rd August 2008

The thing about football seasons is that they play havoc with your life. Holidays had to be suspended and almost everything else put on hold until firstly, the fixtures came out and secondly Sky and then Setanta fiddled about with them to their liking. Football should be played at 3 o'clock on a Saturday afternoon. Having said all of that, when something that has less frequency than Halley's Comet comes around you have to make sure you don't miss any of it, don't you? I had to plan everything down to the tiniest detail to make sure we didn't miss a second of this league campaign. Part of the difficulty was fitting in our annual holiday to Ireland. In the end we decided to go to County Cork between the Blackburn and Wigan games. So before we could cross the Irish Sea we had to negotiate a potentially tricky visit to Blackburn. Their fans had overcome the initial disappointment of losing a very successful manager in Mark Hughes and gaining a relatively inexperienced number one in Paul Ince. They did this by virtue of a very good first day win at Everton. It was obvious that our first away trip in the Premier League would be an even sterner test than our very first game. To further complicate matters for us, Joe's sister Alice wanted to come to the game. Alice is at Manchester University studying History. Joe wanted her to come to the match as well, so to keep them both happy the journey would have to be from Hull to Manchester, on to Blackburn then back to Manchester, on to Bangor for an overnight stay, to Holyhead on Sunday for the ferry to Ireland and the last leg from Dublin to the coast of County Cork. I could feel a migraine coming on. We arrived at Blackburn a good couple of hours before kick off and found some street parking about half a mile away from the ground. All I know about Blackburn is that it is in the north west and was named in 'A Day in the Life' by the Beatles.

Other than that it seems like a fairly ordinary place with a compact town centre and a tidy little train station, pretty much like Hull really. We walked up past Ewood Park to the official away fans pub. It was very refreshing to experience a welcoming atmosphere there. The policy of trying to win over hearts and minds must appease all but the most hostile of football supporters. Thousands of City fans had travelled to Blackburn in good heart and in even better voice. We made our presence felt both outside and inside the ground. I like Ewood Park; it's what a club ground should look like. It has four proper stands and plenty of scope to make a lot of noise. Our fans responded in typical fashion to Paul Duffen's customary visit to us in the away end. To say he is enjoying life as the chairman of Hull City football club, would be a massive understatement.

The City players could not fail to be impressed and buoyed up by the faithful following as we made it seem like a home game. In turn we had to be impressed with our players. To a man they gave everything for the cause against a technically better team. In the end a draw was probably a fair result. Blackburn scored first after Jason Roberts outpaced our defence but within a minute Richard Garcia looped a header beyond the former England number one Robinson, to level the scores. We finished the stronger and I was among the many City fans who honestly thought that we could take it when the fourth official signalled four extra minutes at the end of normal time. In the end I couldn't have been prouder of the team. It seemed like we'd managed to make the kind of start we were all hoping for. Four points from the first two games was a very tidy return for a newly promoted club. The question was would all this effort and industry be enough to keep us in the division? Only time would tell.

After all the travelling we eventually arrived at our holiday home in Durrus in County Cork and found ourselves locked out. We'd tried to contact the owner several times to let her know what time we'd be arriving. We called two or three different numbers and left voicemail messages but she never got back to us. It was dark and we were all cold, tired and hungry so we took the only option left open to us, breaking and entering. Actually we didn't break anything. Our very own artful dodger climbed through an open ground floor window and let us in by finding a key and unlocking the front door. Just as Finn opened up the door the owner rolled up. It could have been an embarrassing situation but in fairness she had ignored our attempts to contact her, so in footballing terms the result was another honourable draw.

Swansea City 2 Hull City 1
Carling Cup 3rd round Tuesday 26th August 2008

The next week was all about eating great food, drinking good wine and beer and generally relaxing. We'd picked the perfect spot for all of that as it turned out, with a remote cottage on the south west coast of Cork. Even there we couldn't fully escape from football though. The big local news in a country dominated by the Gaelic games was that Cork City FC were under examinership. From what I could gather that was very similar to going into administration. As a result the club suffered a ten point deduction. They'd also cut jobs and imposed huge wage reductions. It seems that financial mismanagement is happening everywhere and serves as a sober warning to everyone calling for Paul Duffen to splash the cash without due care and attention.

We had a grand day out in Cork during the week, the birth place of former City stalwart Damien Delaney and the lesser known Roy Keane. I bought a Kilkenny Cats shirt from a local sports store because it was almost exactly the same as our top this season and we had lunch in the English Market. Joanna had seen Rick Stein eat in the market on one of his recent food programmes. He picked tripe and onions from a very good menu and claimed it was one of the best dishes he had ever tasted. Despite coming from a working class, northern city, I've never tried tripe and I thought if it's good enough for Rick, it should be good enough for me. So, passing up the chance to try their excellent Irish stew, I went for the offal. I had the local speciality of drisheen or blood sausage as well. In my neck of the woods that would be a black pudding. While the tripe was bland but just about passable, the drisheen was nothing like black pudding and not recommended for the faint hearted. It was obvious to me that I needed more of the onions and a lot less drisheen and tripe.

"That Rick Stein is a big fecking liar," I said to Joanna in my best Father Ted voice. Tuesday night served up more football as City went into battle at Swansea in the third round of the Carling Cup. I received regular text updates from my mate Dave, none of which seemed very encouraging. A second string line up led from a Dean Windass goal but replies from Pintado and Gomez (beautiful Welsh names) meant that in the end, we went out after extra time. When I watched the highlights on RTE1 that night, I have to say that in comparison to Swansea, we played like a team who have much bigger fish to fry this season. What inevitably awaited me on my return to Hull now though, was the smug face of my little Welsh friend Phil. He is a Swansea Jack to the core, although he has also become infatuated with Chelsea this year, in much the same way as a twelve year old schoolboy might. I'm not sure why he has started following the Blues but it might be something to do with City being in the top flight.

He pointed out that he started following Chelsea when they weren't very good and were actually going through a rough patch. They were sixth in the League at the time. I remember it well, what a terrible week that was.

To say that Phil is annoying is like describing Maradona as a cheat, it doesn't tell you the half of it. I have lost count of the number of times he has told me about Swansea's two seasons in the top flight back in the eighties, or their brief sojourns into Europe. Last season he told me that I would never live to see my team play at Wembley, or win at Wembley, or witness top flight football. If I took the battery out of my watch it would still be right more often than Phil.

Hull City 0 Wigan Athletic 5
Saturday 30th August 2008

After what turned out to be a very relaxing and enjoyable holiday we made the long return Journey back in time to see the next game at the KC. Wigan had lost their first two games despite playing very well. They had never lost their first three in the Premier League though, so it was always going to be tough for us. To make matters worse we would be without Boateng and Gardner through injury. Marlon King couldn't play against the club we had loaned him from, so apart from Geovanni we started with pretty much a Championship side. Things didn't seem quite right for this one and to make matters worse Phil was at the game courtesy of some corporate hospitality. It seems that as far as he is concerned there is such a thing as a free lunch and he was willing to forsake his football principles in order to have one. I decided to have a drink on the concourse. Sadly for me they don't serve the Guinness that I have grown to like so much in recent years and instead only offer the standard fair of bitter and lager. I went for the lager which tasted like the proverbial. I remember reading somewhere recently that actress Sarah Miles drinks her own urine. I can only imagine that she developed the taste for it after downing a pint or two of match day lager.

The game started brightly for us with another sell out crowd, even with Hull FC at Wembley for the Challenge Cup final on the same day. Disaster struck all too early as Myhill and Ricketts conspired to allow an insipid Kilbane corner in for the opening goal. Even my granny could have kept that one out. It just got worse as we made one defensive schoolboy error after another.

We were two down at halftime courtesy of a Valencia strike and five in all. Zaki bagged a brace and looked very good value for it. Even Emile Heskey got on the score sheet. Just how bad could things get? On the face of it we took a right battering but it was a really strange game. Other than the goals Wigan never had a shot. We had a couple of half chances but Kirkland never broke sweat and should have paid to watch as City lacked any real cutting edge. Nobody played that well but sadly our colossus of last season fared the worst. Wayne Brown looked desperately short of pace and was caught out far too many times to mention. It looks as if the Premier League really is a step to far for him.

Finally our match day announcer scored a personal own goal by informing everyone that Hull FC had also lost to St Helens. In front of Wigan fans, what was he thinking? Milo described this as the worst day of his life. Ah, the roller coaster emotions of youth, one day you're up the next you're down. I am far more realistic than him and I was forced to point out,

"It's the worst day of your life so far Milo."

There was an international break now, which meant a week off and chance to iron out the problems in training and hopefully bring in new players before the transfer deadline. It was also a chance to get the absentees fit and ready for the trip to Newcastle for the next match. The media had a field day with this result. Their early predictions must be coming to fruition. We did look out of our depth in this game and everyone was telling us so. If the team learned from it though, then this hammering could possibly serve to make us stronger.

I stayed up late into the night watching the circus that is the transfer window. Along with the fixtures this is another thing that Sky have all stitched up but I suppose that if you sell your soul to the devil then you have to dance to his tune. I watched as three over excitable Sky men, one fresh from presenter school, attempted to whip up the night's proceedings. They showed the same video clips over and over again.

I watched Robinho at Madrid countless times as the clueless trio anticipated his shock move to the nouveau riche

Manchester City. I also saw repetitive grainy footage of Alex Ferguson leading Alistair McGowan out of a meeting room and down a corridor. It turned out to be Dimitar Berbatov the skillful Bulgarian striker not McGowan the talented British mimic. His impending move to the red half of Manchester had dire consequences for our own hopes of landing Fraizer Campbell. Fraizer eventually went to Tottenham as make weight in the Berbatov deal. I just hoped that he wouldn't end up warming the bench at the Lane, the lad deserves much better. All of this just served to illustrate the farcical nature of the game today. Billionaires coming in buying clubs, ridiculous, hyper inflated transfer fees and media frenzy. None of it is good for the fans, or our domestic game, or our national game. Our resident Chelsea fan thinks it is getting out of control. He seems to be ignoring the fact that his beloved oligarch is one of the men who started it all.

By the time the dust had settled we had brought in the very useful looking Rangers and Gabon striker Daniel Cousin to supplement the earlier capture of Guinea defender Kamil Zayette. He had been courted by Everton and Newcastle. We also signed Irish defender Paul McShane from Sunderland on loan. Blimey it's turning in to a right united nations at the KC these days.

Newcastle United 1 Hull City 2
Saturday 13th September 2008

Scientists at the European Organization for Nuclear Research have decided to conduct an experiment that according to many doom mongers could well result in universal destruction. Obviously as you are reading this now you'll be aware that they forgot to put a shilling in the meter and their equipment failed. As a result we got a reprieve and didn't all disappear up our own black hole. However if we had perished at least the Tigers would have remained a Premier League side in perpetuity. I always like to look for a silver lining if I can. I'm definitely more of a 'glass half full' character really.

Kevin Keegan sealed his own fate and did what everyone apart from the Newcastle faithful thought he would do. He walked away from yet another job. To be fair to King Kev though, he must have done so after extreme provocation. He had his role seriously undermined by two of the most ridiculous men in football and in the end this limited but honest man could clearly take no more. All this left the mighty Toon army incensed. How this would effect our forthcoming game was unclear. What was crystal clear was that the Newcastle fans dislike Ashley and Wise with a passion. Only the immediate departure of the hapless duo would ease the rancour of the faithful following.

Phil Brown called for extra security for his players in the run up to the Newcastle game in view of the anticipated protests. This was probably a sensible move as who knows what could happen when thousands of angry Geordies get going. I mean, they marched all the way to London once. Far less sensible was the FA's decision to charge Phil Brown with improper conduct. During the first half of the Wigan game he kicked a water bottle which inadvertently struck the fourth official. It was a shame one of our strikers didn't kick it because it would surely have gone wide of the mark on that day. Phil Brown apologised straight away and volunteered to sit in the stand for the second half. It seems as though this wasn't good enough for the FA. I can only presume that they had finished colouring in down at Soho Square and had to find something else to do in order to while away the long, lonely hours.

Parking in Newcastle, like most big cities is difficult on a Saturday afternoon. We decided to take the easier and more leisurely option of driving to York and catching the train up from there. I was surprised how many Newcastle fans got on board at York and their numbers steadily increased at each stop approaching the city.

We arrived early mainly because, like our manager we didn't know what to expect from the protests. Would there be blockades at the station, picket lines at the club shop and kiosks? I had visions of policeman linking arms struggling to keep the crowds contained a bit like they did with political demonstrators in the sixties and seventies. In reality there was none of this. It appears that the fans are just as unorganised and half hearted as the club itself lately. There was a fair bit of noise outside the ground with anti Ashley and Wise songs and chants. The obligatory derisory T shirts and banners were on display here and there but the whole thing had an amateurish feel about it, again a bit like the club at the moment. As City fans we couldn't help feeling like we were intruding on private grief in some way.

St James' Park is a mightily impressive football stadium, almost slap bang in the city centre. It's built up on two sides and away supporters are perched at the very top of the Sir John Hall stand behind the goal. We had seven levels and fourteen flights of stairs to negotiate. With no Sherpa or oxygen mask supplied, we were forced to complete the long climb unaided.

I have to say it was worth the effort we had to put in. The views of the outlying Geordie countryside were spectacular.

The view of the pitch would be best described as panoramic. Although I couldn't make out the players very well, I was convinced I could clearly see Ant McParlane's forehead. I definitely couldn't see Ashley or Wise though. Apparently the former doesn't feel safe in Newcastle now and as for the latter, well he was never one to take unnecessary risks was he? I remember the Leeds fans invading the pitch when their drop from the Championship was almost confirmed by Ipswich. Little Dennis showed that although his nerve had gone, his legs certainly hadn't as he scampered down the tunnel before the first Leeds fan managed to touch turf.

I noticed a few spare seats around the ground but there were still about 50,000 Geordies who made for some pretty vocal and hostile support. Seriously deluded they may be but nobody could accuse Newcastle fans of being disloyal. They had every intention of getting fully behind their team.

The Newcastle caretaker boss Chris Hughton denied that all the tomfoolery at the club was having an impact on the players. He stated that his team were as well prepared as they could be and should be good enough to win the game. Well much as I admire his bravado, Chris' charges were comprehensively outplayed by a side that have started to look increasingly comfortable in their new surroundings. Marlon King scored his first goals for the club by virtue of a penalty and then a superb solo effort. We actually had the ball in the net three times when Turner headed home only to hear the referees whistle. Quite why the goal was disallowed baffled us all and so instead of killing the game off, the decision seemed to spur on the home side. They pulled one back courtesy of a rebound from the post and a reaction finish from Xisco but the fight back fizzled out as City re-established control of the game and saw it out in some style. To make matters worse for them, Danny Guthrie was dismissed in the closing minutes as he tried to chop Craig Fagan off at the knee.

For us debutant Paul McShane looked assured and the reintroduction of Halmosi and Mendy gave us a makeover even Trinny and Susannah would have been proud of. Ian Ashbee had another outstanding game and should have silenced most of his critics. He looks as confident and assured as the rest of the team. What an achievement to become the only player in European football to captain your side in all divisions of a domestic league.

As we filed out of St James Park and away to the station a few protesters tried to muster one last anti Ashley and Wise demonstration but this faded in the same way as their team had done moments earlier. The train to York or sardine tin as I prefer to call it was absolutely jam packed. A City fan complained and moaned that they should have put on extra carriages for a match day. A Geordie joker came back with a snappy reply.

"All your trains would be empty, living in a dump like Hull man."

The irony that the train was full of people leaving the wonderful city of Newcastle clearly passed over Chubby Brown's scriptwriter.

Gradually the carriages thinned out as the Newcastle fans disembarked at exotic locations like Chester Le Street, Durham and Darlington. We picked up the car at York and headed home to watch Match of the Day, happy and content with our lot.

I did a bit of personal scouting by watching the live game on Sunday as Stoke took on our next opponents Everton. To be honest I wasn't impressed by either side. Stoke's only real attacking threat appears to be the Rory Delap long throw. Although it is some weapon to have in your armoury it means that they are extremely limited. For their part Everton looked slightly better in terms of quality but exhibited the soft underbelly that is their defence with keeper Tim Howard unwilling or unable to command his area. On the face of it we shouldn't have too much to fear from the Toffees. As for November's trip to the land of the giants at Stoke, it also fostered few worries. The kick off for our game was changed to Sunday not at Sky's or Setanta's request but because of the rules governing Everton's earlier European tie. I don't know if it's not one thing these days, it's the other.

As a result of Guthrie's Kung Fu style challenge, Craig Fagan was diagnosed with a broken tibia. He could be out for up to four months and this at a time when he was arguably playing the best football of his life. Still, Guthrie will get three games, so that's fair isn't it? This was assault and it caused Fagan actual bodily harm. Guthrie should face police charges. If I broke someone's leg in the street from a deliberate kick I wouldn't just get a ban for three Saturdays now would I?

Hull City 2 Everton 2
Sunday 21st September 2008

Back at work on Monday I was able to hold bragging rights with Phil as Swansea had gone down 2-0 to Crystal Palace. Of course it slipped my mind that blue is the colour nowadays. According to Mrs Phil I look like Peter Kenyon. They are both obviously spending too much time watching Chelsea lately. I actually look nothing like the erstwhile chief executive, other than the fact that we both sport the same hairstyle. The concept is nothing new to me though. In the past I have been compared to every bald man going. Ross Kemp, that guy from the Jerry Springer show, Ray Wilkins, Pierluigi Collina, Tony who lives next door. The list is endless. It's actually quite ignorant and more than a little insulting to make a connection purely down to one feature. I mean that's like saying a man is annoying just because he's Welsh….Hang on a minute though!

I had to go to London with my job during the week. After I checked into in my hotel I got out the tube map and looked at the logistics of getting to all five of City's games in the capital this season. I worked out that Arsenal, Chelsea and Fulham were relatively easy to get to, while West Ham and Spurs would be a little more troublesome. In truth all of these games would probably prove to be very tricky matches for our boys in black and amber.

I took a stroll later on that evening looking for somewhere to eat. I found a cosy looking Italian just off the Tottenham Court Road. Armed with my copy of the Evening Standard for company I sat down and had some very good spaghetti and a couple of glasses of wine. I read all about how England are good again after our resurgent win in Croatia. I reminded myself sharply that one Swallow doesn't make a summer and that we need to be extradited from the mess the FA has allowed us to get into before we have any real chance of ending forty odd years of hurt. When my work was done the next day I walked to Kings Cross Station along the side streets just off Euston Road. As I stood on a corner waiting for the lights to change, famous writer, actor and one time professional scouser Alexi Sayle, rode by on his bike. I wanted to shout after him, I was going to tell him how much I enjoy his writing and ask him if he was an Everton or Liverpool fan but the moment was gone and so was he. In a speeding grey flash, he slipped the Sturmey Archers into top and disappeared into the distance. It didn't matter, I'm sure my critical assessment of his work wouldn't really bother him. As for his football allegiance, his father was a communist, so I guess he really would have to be a red. I boarded my train loaded up with goodies from The Cyber Candy Store, guaranteeing that the kids would be pleased to see me. I settled down in my seat for the trip back up north to God's county, with Sunday on my mind.

With Fagan playing so well it was disappointing to lose him to injury but having played Craig in a front two in the last game, Phil Brown had a ready made replacement in the shape of Daniel Cousin for Sunday's match. There had been a lot of talk of Everton not firing on all cylinders yet and even being tired from the week's European exertions. I was having none of that, after all this squad finished fifth last term and they had quality all over the pitch. While here was no doubt that this would be our most difficult match to date, it was still one we could win. Arriving at the ground early I went through the turnstiles with Finn and Joe, leaving Joanna to bring up the rear. Once inside I looked at Joe's pass book. I was sure that he had a photo in it now, it must have fallen out. When Joanna didn't appear I realised what I had done. I'd picked up last years passes by mistake, leaving the current ones on the bookshelf back home. I looked through the gap in the exit gates and saw Joanna outside reaching for her phone. Calling her over to me I could see she wasn't best pleased. I had to admit that if I had been on the other side I wouldn't have been very happy either. Obviously the ticket number corresponded to a game we'd missed last year. We had caught the turnstile operator dozing and unfortunately she hadn't. The look on her face was priceless.

"Just go round to the ticket office and explain what's happened," I said.

"They're bound to let you in."

As Joanna wandered off I couldn't help having a little chuckle to myself. Within a few minutes she had joined us on the concourse. She had a face like thunder but with no harm done and a drink in her hand, Joanna did manage to see the funny side and calm down.

The match was yet another sell out. A full away allocation accompanied by very vocal support for both sides helped to create equal amounts of excitement and tension. City started the game with pace, passion and no little skill. We maintained the good form that we had shown at Newcastle a week earlier and continued to look like a side comfortable in the Premier League. The starting eleven looked fluent and assured as they controlled the first hour of the game. Some of the football was superb, probably the best we had seen so far. Turner thundered in a header from a corner to give us the lead and we forced Phil Neville into a very characteristic own goal early in the second half to make it two. I was dying for the announcer to say,

"Scoring his first goal for Hull City, number eighteen Philip Neville!" Sadly he never did.

At this point we were cruising. I work with an Everton fan who was sat in the north stand for the match. I sent Gary three or four texts pilling on the agony and just like his beloved Toffees he offered no reply. This was looking good. Perhaps we would keep a clean sheet for the first time. With twenty five minutes to go surely it was time to bring back Boateng, go four five one and stifle the life out of the game. Everton's quality started to show through now as Lescott and Saha, who were both introduced at half time, began to run the show at either end of the pitch. A goal seemed inevitable and it came as Cahill's shot rebounded off the crossbar and over the line. Still no Boateng and yet still more pressure from Everton.

Osman scored the equaliser we were all expecting and then Boateng came on and we finally went four five one. We managed to hold on for a draw but I could see the headlines in the morning papers, 'Tigers choke on Toffees.' Maybe it's a sign of how far we've come but it felt like two points dropped and this against an established Premier League club who have spent more time in the top flight than anyone else. The Everton fan sent me a mocking text. I thought it was strange that Gary had found his phone now. As we trudged away The Clash's 'London Calling' blasted from the stadium speakers. Just what you need on the back of a disappointment I thought, a trip to North London's finest.

It turned out that Greek international Stelios was at the game; apparently he was casting an eye over his prospective new team mates. The bad news for me is that as a fellow bald man he adds to Mrs Phil's already substantial list of people I can be confused with. The Greek duly signed, swelling our international contingent even more. Back at work we went through the usual post match analysis but in truth I had other things on my mind. The company I work for is undergoing a major reorganisation. As everyone knows this is business speak for job cuts. I had picked voluntary redundancy as one of my options but it was still a strange feeling. I never thought I would be working in the same place for twenty four years but now that I had, it seemed like a very big part of my life to let go. Still as one door closes another one slams in your face, as they say. I was confident of moving on and if not I could stay at home, bake bread and look after Joe.

Arsenal 1 Hull City 2
Saturday 27th September 2008

I've been to the Emirates once before. I got hold of a couple of tickets for the Arsenal versus Tottenham Carling Cup semi final last season, courtesy of a mate who is a Spurs fan. He got the tickets only to find he couldn't go himself. Never one to look a gift horse in the mouth, I saw it as a chance to visit another ground, perhaps one I would never see with my own side. Little did I know, eh?

It was a midweek game so I drove to Peterborough with Finn and from there we took a train which would stop at Finsbury Park. We should then have a short stroll to the ground. I could see the impressive Stadium looming in the distance as the train slowed on the approach to Finsbury. Unfortunately, although the train slowed the driver clearly had no intention of stopping. We had boarded the wrong train, next stop Kings Cross and we would have to jump on to the tube to get back up to the ground. Time to kick off was getting very tight.

"We can still make it," I said to Finn as we ran down the platform. Sadly the Met's finest had other ideas. We were directed to Euston, away from the severely overcrowded tube at Kings Cross. As we marched with a small army of Gooners towards Euston a similar sized group of Arsenal fans met us coming the other way. Euston was closed as well. Only one thing for it, dash across to Russell Square and board the tube there. We made it just, only just in time for the kick off. I had no intention of repeating that night's episode. We would allow plenty of time to see City take on Wenger's men. The bookies were offering very generous odds against us getting a draw and ridiculous odds on overturning the Gunners. I fought the urge to put a tenner on us winning; the trip was pricey enough as it was. It's not that I don't have faith in my team but you have to be realistic. Only West Ham had beaten Arsenal in their new surroundings. So while I lived in hope, I had to admit that our chances of getting anything from the game were slim at best. Anyway I remember my dad telling me that you never see a bookie on a bike.

As good as the Emirates stadium is it's not perfect. When we came before we were sat right in the corner and from there we couldn't see all the way down the line into the other end. We had no such problem this time as our seats were on the back row of the bottom tier and further down the pitch. We had a perfect view of proceedings although, because of the overhang from the tier above we couldn't see scoreboard. Our three thousand supporters were once again magnificent in helping to create a fantastic atmosphere. I think so many of us were there to simply enjoy the occasion. Only the foolish or plain drunk could imagine us getting a result against Arsenal in their own back yard.

The Gunners quickly settled into their rhythm and started to play some sublime stuff. In fact at times it was bordering on the ridiculous. It was like playing the Harlem Globetrotters I thought, as clever pass followed clever trick, time after time.

In spite of all of this we really didn't look out of place and it didn't seem like we were here just to make up the numbers as the pundits had expected. Phil Brown started with a four, three, three formation, with Geovanni playing in the hole. We were definitely going for the result. Our fans went through the complete repertoire of songs from the obvious 'Just Like A Library' to the more obscure 'Fish Out, Dolan Out,' harking back to our darker days. One particularly over excitable lad two rows in front jumped up and down waving his arms like a whirling dervish for almost the entire half. He seemed to lack the very basics of muscle coordination but you couldn't knock his enthusiasm. I was sure he would have someone's eye out before too much longer.

"I'd love to play him at Operation," said Finn.

We were level at the break and we certainly deserved to be. I didn't know how much longer we could hold out though. Surely we would fade having already covered so many yards and so many blades of grass to contain Arsenal's gifted stars. Finn and Joe kept themselves amused by wrapping their scarves around there heads like Bedouin tribesmen. The mood of the rest of the City faithful was equally good. There was a definite buzz around the away section. Spirits were high and we all hoped however unrealistic, for a favourable end to the evening. Arsenal had other ideas as they broke through early in the second half with some very precise passing movements. They almost walked the ball into the net and ended up forcing the unfortunate McShane into an own goal. We took a collective sharp intake of breath, fearing the worst and bracing ourselves for the floodgates to open.

Buoyed by our amazing support the team held firm and steadied the ship. I was beginning to think that we could keep the score to a respectable level and then the magic moment came. Geovanni picked up the ball on the left, shaped up and from fully twenty five yards or maybe more he unleashed an inch perfect wonder strike past the despairing Almunia in to the top corner of the Arsenal goal. The City faithful erupted almost lifting off the roof. Who'd have thought it, little Hull City coming back to snatch an improbable draw? Well obviously none of the City players thought it because shortly afterwards Cousin leapt high above the Arsenal defence to power home the winning goal. The young disjointed Dervish in front of us went into overdrive. I was convinced more than ever that he would do himself or someone else an injury before the night was out. All the fans went wild. Let's face it days like these don't come along too often, so we had to make the most of it. We mocked Arsenal and praised City in equal measure but the highlight came with the infamous 'Mauled by the Tigers,' complete with clawing actions. It was pure high camp and worth every glorious moment to see fifty odd thousand puzzled Gooners stare back in disbelief. As we left the stadium I could have sworn I saw the guy from the betting kiosk putting his bike clips on.

I called David Burns at Radio Humberside after the game as we hung around, milking every last drop of atmosphere from this wonderful evening. Burnsy asked me for another superlative to describe City's historic performance. Incredible was all I could think of but that would do. To come behind and win against possibly the best footballing side in the country at their own ground was truly incredible. We went across the road for a drink while we waited for the crowd and the inevitable tube station crush to clear. At one side of the ground the name Arsenal is sculpted in huge concrete letters. I got Finn and Joe to sit on the R and S and with some careful framing and skilful camera work; I was able to take a souvenir snap of the boys posing on the word ARSE in front of the stadium. It wasn't big and it certainly wasn't clever but I was satisfied that our work here was done.

Our train back to Hull wasn't until late afternoon on Sunday so after we had breakfast we took Finn and Joe to the science museum for a look round. I was last there on a school trip to Wembley for the Challenge Cup Final in 1976. I think St Helens won back then. Some things never change. I remember it being an event packed day. Apart from the game we had lunch at Lyons Corner House, visited the science museum and took in a show at The Palladium. Bruce Forsyth was doing his one man show at the famous old theatre. I think this was his pre rug wearing, Anthea Redfern period. He made the mistake of trying to interact with the audience, asking where people were from and the like. Of course he was greeted by about thirty northern school kids chanting "ull, ull, ull" non stop from the cheap seats. I think it spoiled his evening. I'm sure the Arsenal fans know how he felt. The only thing I recognised in the

Science museum was an automatic door first introduced in 1933. Joe found it wasn't working and I seem to remember it wasn't working back in 1976 either. Like I said, some things never change. We caught the tube back to Kings Cross. On the way down a connecting corridor Finn spotted Evan Davis, the presenter of Dragons Den. This happens to be one of his favourite programmes, I don't know why.

Sharp as a tack Finn stuck his hand out towards Evan.

"I'll shake your hand for eighty percent equity, you know it makes sense," Finn said to the baffled and bemused Presenter.

Tottenham Hotspur 0 Hull City 1
Sunday 5th October 2008

Spurs appeared to be shambolic at this time. They had shipped out the foundation of a very good side and brought in highly rated individuals who are not performing as a team. They are not used to being at the wrong end of the table and have a Spanish manager who is under pressure and rapidly falling out of love with the English game. With all that in mind it would appear that we had very little to fear from our swift return to the capital. Appearances can be deceptive though and it was incumbent on all of us to forget the glory of the Arsenal game and concentrate on the very hard task of getting back to back wins. Nobody at Tottenham, least of all Ramos would want to follow their North London neighbours in being mauled by the Tigers. The game was on Sunday, again to allow Spurs to recover from their Thursday night European exertions. We drove straight down to London and parked at our hotel. The weather was shocking and it just seemed easier than messing about with train connections, especially as we needed to get straight back after the game on Sunday. We had our own pre match meal on Saturday evening at an Indian restaurant just round the corner from the hotel. The food and service was very good, sadly I couldn't say the same about the manners of the group at the next table. We were forced to endure four very loud and very ignorant Americans yawping their way through dinner. The loudest and fattest of the group was especially rude to the staff.

"Hey buddy where's the food?" He yelled at the waiter.

"Just coming sir."

"Yeh and so is Christmas," he replied to the increasingly harassed waiter.

His fellow diners howled with laughter as if he had just told the best joke ever.

"He is so funny," I whispered to Joanna.

"Steve Martin must be panicking back in LA."

Although this guy thought he was so funny and even though he thought he knew everything, he obviously wasn't aware that you should never, ever upset restaurant staff before they serve the food. I wondered what our genial hosts could do to exact revenge on the bullet headed Yanks. I imagined cases of Delhi belly all round as they greedily stuffed themselves with unfeasibly large amounts of spicy Indian food.

Getting up bright and early on Sunday morning, the first thing I noticed was that it was still raining; we were going to get very wet. We took the over ground train from Liverpool Street to White Hart Lane station. From there it's a short walk to the ground itself. There was a delay getting into the stadium as the turnstiles remained closed. The only thing I could think of as we got wetter still was a pitch inspection; surely they wouldn't call off the game at this late stage would they? The last time I fell fowl of this particular situation was last season's visit to Colchester. I went alone on Tiger Travel and the rain was also torrential on that day. We got the message that the match had been called off about ten miles from Layer Road, just in time for the driver to sail majestically round a roundabout and head back north. The best we could muster by way of entertainment that day was haranguing club mascot Roary into donning his uniform and doing a turn at Grantham services. It was to say the least, a thoroughly miserable day. It seemed that luck and referee Rob Styles was on our side now though, as the turnstiles opened allowing us to enter a very soggy White Hart Lane. Tottenham's famous old ground has been updated and modified but the golden cockerel still stands proudly high above the main stand presiding over the clubs current crop of stars.

Paul Duffen has been a Spurs supporter since his childhood but there would be no divided loyalties today. Hull City is now very much his club. I had no doubt that he would put aside his first love and get fully behind the Tigers. In addition to Dean Marney making a return to his old club the connections continued with the first league start for Hull City's star of last season, Frazier Campbell. Clearly Ramos was working on the, old player returning to haunt his former club rule. Leading up to kick off I was significantly more nervous than a week earlier at the Emirates. If we played as well as we could then I thought we could do a North London double but it wasn't going to be straight forward. Tottenham didn't want to have the ignominy of their worst start since 1912.

I've recently started sporting a beard in support of Matt Duke and the Everyman testicular cancer appeal. I think it makes me look a bit like an explorer, or a submarine commander. The kid's think it makes me look like a geography teacher. My facial hair seems to have coincided with City's exceptional run of form and while I do not believe in coincidence, I am very superstitious. I'm from a very superstitious family. It's very Pagan and very common in Hull. As a result I never walk under ladders or spill salt without throwing some over my shoulder. I also never walk straight through a house and….the list is endless. So while City are doing well the beard stays.

We were perched up in the corner behind the goal at Spurs and in full view of a futuristic police observation post. I say futuristic but only if your ideas of technology come from watching repeats of seventies cult classic 'Space 1999.'

From there the boys in blue can keep an eagle eye on away supporters, even if their time would been at least as well spent watching the Tottenham fans on our right. I have to say that for the neutral observer watching the game, this was probably our most exciting match so far. End to end stuff with both sides getting their share of the opening exchanges. We were first to break the deadlock with a free kick awarded about twenty five yards out from the Spurs goal. Geovanni stood to the left of the ball and Dawson closer on the right. There was only ever going to be one person taking the kick and only ever going to be one place the ball would end up. Geovanni obliged with consummate ease to send the onion bag bulging, while fellow countryman Gomes could only look on with equal amounts of admiration and disappointment. Our talented Brazilian seems to be conducting a goal of the season competition with himself. The second half saw us go to a four, five, one formation and defend manfully if a little too deeply for my liking against a Spurs attack who were clearly giving it everything they had. For all the pressure we defended exceptionally well, trying to hit Tottenham on the break whenever we could. In truth we were reasonably comfortable.

The final whistle brought a mass exodus of Spurs fans that had started with a steady trickle at least five minutes earlier. Only the ecstatic City fans remained to sing and cheer their heroes on their way. Frazier Campbell cut a forlorn figure on the pitch. He shook hands with old friends, while chants of 'You should have stayed with a big club,' rang around the fast emptying White Hart Lane. Our astounding start continued and meanwhile Spurs did indeed have their worst start since the year the Titanic sank. I swear I could see the golden cockerel shake his head in disbelief. We sang on, ever louder while Juande Ramos stood crestfallen in the same way that Bruce Forsyth had done years earlier at the hands of his tormentors from Hull.

As we waited in the long queue at the station to get back to Liverpool Street, we were kept entertained by a lovable old Londoner. He harped on about us not having electricity in Hull and the fact that we actually inhabit a fishing village in the north east. I never realised that Dan Kieran's dad was a Tottenham fan. We went our separate ways to different platforms but not before I had chance to thank the old soak for the points. He replied by wishing us a safe and comfortable journey home or at least I think that was the gist of his parting message.

I quite enjoy my visits to the capital, especially lately. I do like to get back home though and once out of the London, there is something very comforting and extremely satisfying about driving up the Great North Road. I tuned into Talksport to hear Phil Brown chat to Jason Cundy and Micky Quinn. While they and many others are genuinely surprised by Hull City's impressive start to life in the Premier League, most Tigers fans aren't. That evening Hull City sat third in the Premier League after seven games. These were unprecedented times, heady days. An all time highest league position and the third best ever start by a newly promoted club in Premier League history. This was our reward for all the hard work everyone had put in.

Nobody, least of all me was taking anything for granted though. Our aim was still to survive in this league and anything else would be a bonus but there was no denying this was one hell of a start. Another international break beckoned, coming at just the right time if you ask me. It's a chance to rest, to regroup and to prepare for our next game. I wonder how long it will be before we have a current England international in the team though. My money's on Michael Turner, the way he's going, it shouldn't be too long. The newspapers the next day were more about how bad Tottenham were instead of how good we are. This is a familiar pattern now but what else could the media luvvies do? Admit they were wrong about us? No not on your life. It would be far better to put our outstanding start and stratospheric league position down to our opposition having off days. That's all of them except Wigan then. As a matter of fact even Wigan didn't play well, according to manager Steve Bruce.

A couple of days later I was back in London again, not for football this time though. I do some work with the Tallow Chandlers. They are an ancient livery company who have links with industry and equally strong connections to the army. I was invited to a dinner to mark the centenary of the Territorial Army and never one to refuse a kind offer, I headed back down south.

I arrived at my hotel early, so that I could get ready for the evening. I checked out my appearance in mirror. It was no good; I still looked like a bit like a doorman. It's the hair you see, while I have no real problem with being bald, I have to accept that it is very unfortunate in certain respects.

Yes I save money on shampoo, I stay cool in the summer and I don't need to worry about going grey. I invariably get compared to practically every bald man alive though and I can never fully escape the bouncer tag. I went to a game at Chesterfield once and I asked a rival fan where the nearest pub was. The slack jawed youth spoke.

"Down the road about two hundred yards on the left but they have bouncers on the door."

"You're not a bouncer are you?" He continued "I hate bouncers; you look a bit like a bouncer, no offence pal."

I let out a long sigh and shook my head.

"No it's a mystery illness, just woke up one day and there it was, gone." I carried on.

"Like her on the telly, you know, Gail Porter."

The youth looked stunned. I turned in the direction of the pub. He spluttered apologies at me as I walked away.

"It's ok," I said "it's an easy mistake to make, happens all the time, the doctor said it might grow back one day."

It was a harsh thing to do and I regretted it a bit afterwards but I get so fed up of sweeping generalisations coming my way.

The dinner turned out to be very enjoyable. The guy next to me moaned about the state of the economy and the impending financial crisis. He told me that it had all the makings of the worst he could ever remember. He looked older than Bobby Robson, so things must be bad. His solution to get us out of this mess was an interesting and radical one. He would sack everyone from all of the thousands of new jobs Labour had created since 1997. If he was a footballer I'm sure he would be a right winger. I suppose his reasoning was understandable though. He had over a million in the bank and the government only guarantee the first £50,000 of anyone's cash. These are worrying times for rich and poor alike.

My mind wandered a bit and I thought about football again. A table had just been published showing each club's debt in the Premier League. Hull City are at the top of the table with only £200,000 worth of debt while Chelsea and Manchester United prop it up with the thick end of £1 billion at risk. West Ham seemed to be teetering on the edge of the abyss, having first lost their shirt sponsor through bankruptcy and then possibly their owner in the Iceland bank collapse. They also face stumping up a fine of around £30 million in favour of Sheffield United for the Tevez and Mascherano debacle. There is even talk of Sheffield players suing individually for lost earnings as a result of being relegated from the Premier League. If West Ham go bust they could be the first of many.

With the meal finished the Tallow Chandler Master stood to make a speech. Unfortunately for him, the microphone kept cutting out which meant he sounded just like Hull's very own Norman Collier. I expected him to ruffle his hair, slip his jacket back over his shoulders and jump up on to the top table. I thought he might go on to act like a chicken, in a bid to recreate Norman's other joke. Unfortunately for me he was handed a replacement microphone and finished his speech with his feathers decidedly unruffled.

Hull City 1 West Ham United 0
Sunday 19th October 2008

England were due to play Kazakhstan on Saturday. Unfortunately like a lot of English football fans, I have little interest in my national side these days. Well listen, the England players didn't come to see me when I was bad did they? In truth, there is much more to it than that. Our collective apathy stems from years of mismanagement of our national game. The blame for this rests squarely at the feet of the Football Association. Everything that is wrong with English football is because the FA has allowed it to happen. Still now, they don't learn. Recently UEFA chief Michel Platini warned that we are in grave danger of losing our national identity. If a Frenchman, who let's be honest has no love for the English, issues such a stark warning, maybe we should sit up and take notice.

Unfortunately FA Premier League chief, Richard Scudamore doesn't think Platini is right and he dismissed the Frenchman's claims as nonsense. He seemingly prefers to concentrate his efforts on resurrecting his ridiculous 39th game idea. So England can be crap for another fifty years but as long as we have mouth watering ties like Wigan versus Bolton in Singapore, everything will be fine. Until the situation improves I will not waste time following England. I will wait instead to see which tabloid is first to use a side splitting 'Borat' reference. England initially made hard work of it but ultimately ran out comfortable 5-1 winners to ensure that the papers would not be too unkind. On the home front Geovanni won goal of the month for his wonder strike against Arsenal and Phil Brown won the manager of the month award. People were beginning to notice us. Maybe other teams would start taking us more seriously now after all. England made it four wins out of four as they eased past Belarus 3-1 in Minsk We seemed to be doing rather well without our regular England captain. I try to get a little of my own back with the Welshman by having a go at the illustrious Chelsea man. Solely for Phil's benefit I claim that John Terry is typical of everything that is wrong with the modern game, in fact everything that is wrong in our celebrity obsessed, greed driven society. While his team-mates sweated for the cause in some far flung corner of the former Soviet empire, Old JT probably sat in his stately home counting his money. It was a distinct possibility that he selected a hand rolled Cuban cigar and proceeded to light it with a crisp £50 note. Later he would more than likely take a stroll to his cavernous wine cellar in order to select a bottle of vintage Champagne. Meanwhile his adoring wife would perhaps forgo the baby Bentley in favour of jumping onto her prize unicorn and cantering down The Kings Road. She might shop for yet more ridiculously expensive designer clobber from yet another ridiculously lavish boutique. I'm only joking of course; we all know that there are no such things as Unicorns.

The West Ham match seemed like yet another game or to be more precise another team we were due to play at exactly the right time. All the financial pressures that the Hammers were under would surely impact on the playing staff. As I always say, the Tigers still need to be at their best and I'm sure Phil and the team would ensure no complacency crept in. I also have to say though; we really do seem to be getting the rub of the green at the moment. This was yet another Sunday game. Not this time because of Sky or any of the other TV overlords. It wasn't because West Ham are involved in Europe. I can't believe I have just written that. No, it was because of Hull Fair. Once again our football team, now a Premier League team mind you, had to give way for a travelling fair because we live next door to the site they use. The fair has surely run its course at its present location. I know it's traditional and the kids love it and all that but I just think it's time it moved, preferably to Leeds or Sheffield or anywhere else really.

I sincerely hope that Paul Duffen and his colleagues can work with the council and develop the land around the stadium. A hotel, a casino, apartments, or even retail outlets, would all be infinitely preferable to the fair. I'm sure I seem like a bit of a killjoy and probably out of step with a lot of people from Hull but I hate the whole shabby, annual excuse to pick your pockets. As my granddad quite rightly used to say, there's nowt fair about the fair. The only positive about switching the game to Sunday was that we had an extra day to prepare and this would be especially important as we had nine players away on international duty during the league break. Nine players, think of it, Hull City had nine players away with their national sides at the same time.

Looking at the newspapers the results from Saturday had altered the look of the Premier League. It now appeared more normal with all four of the big boys in place. I'm sure football authorities, writers, sports editors, presenters and pundits all over England agree.

Inside the KC stadium Tigers eyes looked menacingly from the scoreboard in the north stand. Underneath the legend read, 'Living The Dream.' That is exactly what we are doing in Hull at the moment and not even a full away contingent of genuine, battle hardened Eastenders could spoil our day. West Ham are like a poor mans Arsenal. They play a good passing game and keep possession well but they are decidedly one paced and from early on looked incapable of breaking our well drilled lines. They did have the ball in the net though as Ilunga cheekily flicked the ball overhead from Myhill's hands. Despite manager Gianfranco Zola complaining bitterly that the goal should have stood, the laws of the game are unequivocal. The ball was in the goalkeepers control and as such unplayable by the West Ham defender. Referee Chris Foy correctly ruled foul play and duly booked the player for his trouble.

The game looked very much like a goalless draw to me as neither side seemed capable of providing the killer punch. Enter Michael Turner to add further weight towards his international credentials. Yet again he proved he was quite literally head and shoulders above another England centre back in Matthew Upson. Turner powered home a header directly from an Andy Dawson corner to burst West Hams bubble and claim all three points. What's more, we were back in third spot in the table. We seem intent on gate crashing the party at the moment and we are only behind Nottingham Forest in having the best ever start by a newly promoted Premier League side.

Jimmy Greaves famously once said that football is a funny old game. I'm sure he isn't laughing now as one of his former club's West Ham, had fallen to us and another Tottenham, languish at the foot of the league. Meanwhile unfashionable, much maligned Hull City sit amongst the big boys, that's what I call funny. Talksport's Ian Abrahams, or as he is more fittingly known Moose, claimed that his very own happy hammers shouldn't have lost to Hull.

"Even the Hull fans said we should have been about three up at halftime," he told a less than enthralled Alan Brazil. He continued to bleat on.

"If only they had taken their chances."

Abrahams is yet another in a long line of bitter so called experts who refuse to admit that they could possibly be wrong about the Tigers. Only David Mellor has backed down. He even issued an apology to us for his earlier remarks. Perhaps he is a gentleman after all. Again I find it all very funny.

What's not at all amusing is an unsavoury element creeping back into the game just now. Saturday saw trouble between rival hooligans at the Millwall v Leeds game.

Elsewhere a thug at Aston Villa decided to throw a coin of the realm, narrowly missing Harry Redknap but felling the unfortunate linesman in the process. West Ham's finest also decided to part with their hard earned in similar fashion at our place, picking out the east stand faithful as targets. There were also one or two skirmishes in Walton Street after the game. On field activities seemed little better. Joey Barton faced the media and made a statement about how he had learned his lesson following his brief detention at Her Majesty's pleasure. He claimed to realise he had made mistakes but he would be putting that all behind him and not wasting his last chance. He has made mistakes? Putting diesel in your car instead of petrol is a mistake. Leaving home without your wallet is a mistake. Beating someone senseless is very much a choice and not a mistake. By choosing to be a thug Barton should lose the right to anymore chances, it's as simple as that. The football authorities have worked hard to put their house in order after the dark days of the seventies and eighties. The game is now very much a family orientated one and nobody wants to see it slip back into the mire, it's time for action down at FA headquarters.

Now definitely wasn't a time to spoil our happy hour though. We should bask in our glory and marvel at the fact that West Ham win made the score London 0 Hull 4. This really is a good place to be and you can believe it.

West Bromwich Albion 0 Hull City 3
Saturday 25th October 2008

I have always found our trips to the Black Country reasonably enjoyable. Although our results have been mixed over the years we do seem to be getting the hang of it down there, as last seasons excellent win against the Baggies illustrates.

Thinking back the game against West Brom last term was a seminal moment. It was an indication to City followers that we were on the up and that we could compete with the so called quality clubs of the Championship and maybe beyond.

I remember seeing West Brom's celebrity fan outside the Hawthorns. No not Frank Skinner the other one, Adrian Chiles. He was walking towards me through the crowd so I moved to shake his hand as if I had just seen a long lost friend.

"Now then," I said.

"Hi," he replied.

"Nice shirt," he continued pointing at my Led Zep T shirt.

"Err nice to see you too," I said as I noticed he was wearing a ridiculously tight pink, Lyle and Scott golf jumper.

I quite like the affable Match Of The Day Two presenter. He's fairly knowledgeable, he has an easy manner and reminds me very much of a young Benny Hill to look at. I have to say he blotted his copybook at the start of the season though. He got excited about City coming up through the play offs but only because he saw us as a team his beloved Albion could beat in order to help them survive. I'm quite sure in the lead up to this season's match he must have looked at the table and wondered if he had been too hasty in condemning us. The Hawthorns is another traditional football ground which has been updated but retains the atmosphere, thanks in the main to some pretty fanatical support. It's also the highest ground above sea level in England, as any keen trivia quiz goer will tell you.

Driving down to the Midlands takes about two and a half hours and it's easily manageable in a day. I have a pretty good Sat Nav so I tend to let that do all the work. It has been a godsend. It's stopped all the rows we used to have on the road when Joanna tried to read the map. It must be a women thing because I remember regularly taking the front seat alongside my dad on long family outings. In all honesty there are so many things that Joanna is much better at than me, so I don't worry about the maps too much. The old Sat Nav isn't foolproof though, as this old fool can testify. We were on our way to Coventry a couple of seasons ago and we ended up in the middle of a housing estate instead of at the Ricoh arena. Little did I know the Sat Nav was using old maps and had directed us to the scene of Coventry's former glories at Highfield Road.

I took a few minutes to go and look at the Jeff Astle Gates outside the ground. I liked Jeff, he was an honest old fashioned centre forward a bit like Chris Chilton but I will never forgive him for missing a sitter against Brazil in the 1970 World Cup. The gates are a fitting tribute to the Albion legend even if his image did look a little like an A level art project. Looking in the programme before the match I noticed an article by former City player Richard Sneeks. Of course he is something of an Albion legend himself and now works for the club. He praised City for their achievements and although he was as surprised as everyone else by our meteoric start, he always thought that we were a big club in waiting and were capable of making it to the top flight.

The match itself reminded me a lot of the Spurs game. There was a frenetic pace and it was absolutely wide open. West Brom looked the better side and certainly had the better chances. Hoefkens hit the woodwork early on and both Miller and Bednar came close to scoring. They had more possession, more chances, more corners, in fact more of everything except goals and like the Spurs game we rode our luck a bit but defended very well. It was goalless at halftime and I got the feeling that West Brom's failure to capitalise would be to our benefit. So it was, as we swept them aside with a slick counter attacking display after the break. Zayette was first to score when he volleyed in from a Marney corner. He was promptly rewarded for his effort by Cousin, who clothes lined him in an over exuberant goal celebration. Thankfully no harm was done. Well worked finishes from Geovanni and King completed the rout, leaving the City fans ecstatic. We sang our hearts out as always but this time we premiered a new song. 'We Are Top of the League' echoed around the Hawthorns as dejected Albion fans threw the towel in and headed home early.

That evening we stood level on points with Liverpool and Chelsea at the summit of the Premier League. Of course the pundits said all the right things but you could tell it was killing them to admit they could possibly be wrong about us. I wish I had a pound for every time Alan Hansen referred back to the Wigan game and said that he feared for us. Fellow Scot Andy Gray looked like he was sucking a lemon over on Sky as he heaped faux praise on the Tigers. I suspect that what he really wanted to say was that we had done well for a little club but Chelsea and United would sort us out soon enough and normal service would be resumed.

Let's face it this wasn't the way the script was supposed to go. Sky executives must be passing kidney stones at the mere thought of the Tigers spoiling the party.

Hull City 0 Chelsea 3
Wednesday 29th October 2008

I had already started to look at the foot of the table and wonder who would go down this season. Of course at this stage it could still be us. Amongst the usual suspects Spurs of course, were in very big trouble. The only way they could save themselves was to completely clear the decks and get a motivational manager to make their talented ensemble click. Stand up Harry Redknapp. In an audacious and utterly surprising move, Daniel Levy sacked Ramos and installed the crafty Cockney. The Spurs fans were delighted and rightly so. If Redknapp couldn't save them, no one could. The Pompey faithful were less pleased. I think it will be a very cold day in hell before Harry is welcome on the south coast again. This is the transient nature of the modern game. Everything changes I suppose, it's just that Redknapp seems to have no conscience when looking at the colour of the grass on the other side of the fence. I hope and trust that our own man at the helm will show more loyalty because he seems to be attracting attention for all the right reasons just now.

Ahead of the Chelsea game workplace rivalry stepped up a gear. I mocked the Welshman for Chelsea's surrender to Liverpool. In turn he typically switched allegiance to Swansea seeing that they had registered a fine win over Southampton at the weekend. Phil had some how managed to get tickets for the Chelsea game in their end. Oh I remember he's one of their biggest fans now, isn't he?

"I hope you get a nice warm welcome from the East Stand," I said. This would be another tough game. We could face the dreaded backlash but Liverpool did show the way to beat the Blues and I'm sure Phil Brown was taking note. In any event City should make it harder for them than our last encounter. We faced Chelsea in the Carling Cup last season and in all honesty we were in awe of them. We showed them far too much respect and treat the game more like a party than an actual contest. Paul Duffen pushed the boat out blowing the entire entertainment budget on pyrotechnics. Sadly the only football fireworks came from the Blues as they beat us soundly on the night. We now have a different team and an entirely different mentality. There was no reason to fear the Fulham Road Millionaires. It was a cold, crisp evening down at the KC stadium, I just hoped that we could make the visit of our illustrious opponents especially frosty.

The away allocation was full due to the fact that Chelsea's Russian owner forked out for travel to entice his fans to venture north. On Chelsea TV, host Gigi had warned the supporters that it would be cold up in Hull.

"Remember to wrap up warm," she informed them. I think that she may also have told them to be careful on the ice and keep a look out for polar bears. Obviously geography is not the forte of the pretty but vacuous presenter. Hull is in England, not just south of the North Pole.

Within three minutes of the kick off Frank Lampard collected a soft ball on the edge of our area and either through sheer brilliance or plain good luck placed the ball exactly where Boaz couldn't get it, to put Chelsea one up. An already big ask was made even more difficult, it was going to be a long night. Credit to our players though, they stuck to their game plan. They tried to keep their shape and play football. We had one or two good chances to draw level, most notably when Cousin showed neat feet to make space on the edge of Chelsea's area and thunder a shot against the base of post.

Unfortunately that was as good as it got. After the break Larry, Curly and Mo, sorry I meant to say Turner, Zayette and Myhill, failed to clear an easy ball. The comedy defending allowed Anelka a simple shot to an empty net for the second killer goal.

That was that, as Chelsea controlled the rest of the game with Malouda getting the inevitable third on the break as we pressed forward in search of something. Dean Windass was introduced with ten minutes to go but even this legend of a man couldn't perform the heroics necessary to salvage anything from the match. Scolari and Terry said some nice things about Hull City after the game but it's very easy to be gracious in victory and we felt like little boys who had just been patted on the head.

Everyone was now talking about reality checks but I really don't know why. We have always had a keen sense of reality in Hull unlike the latte quaffing toffs from SW6. The Tigers had faced the second best team in Europe and been outplayed but not disgraced. We would go to Manchester to face the best team in Europe with that same sense on Saturday, take our lumps if needs be and then get back to real business in the league.

It's common knowledge that there is a gulf in class between the top four teams and everyone else at the moment. It is not a level playing field and it certainly isn't fair but we are proud to support Hull City and we are happy in the knowledge that it is our team and not just some rich mans plaything.

Manchester United 4 Hull City 3
Saturday 1st November 2008

As well as Alice being at university in Manchester, Joanna's sister Pamela lives in Chorlton Cum Hardy, a trendy suburb of the city. We decided to get across early to visit Pam, Alex and the kids. It was also Finn's fifteenth birthday. Alice had promised to show him the delights of Manchester. He willingly gave his match ticket up for Milo so that he could hang out with Alice and her cool friends for the day. This would be the biggest crowd we had played in front of after Wembley and added to the world class players against us, it would be an extremely stern test. Alex Ferguson had upped the anti even more by telling his players to go out and score plenty of goals against us in order to build up their goal difference. This had all the makings of a very long afternoon. Within three minutes we were victim of some lethal finishing by Ronaldo to go one nil down. We didn't panic though and soon were level from a Cousin header. United stepped up a gear again and restored their lead. Carrick shot in off the post at the same side of the goal Ronaldo had used to good effect earlier. The Portuguese player showed he was no one trick pony by heading home to make it 3-1 at halftime. The city fans kept going throughout and showed undying spirit and keen humour by singing about the fact that we'd never won anything at all. To be honest we were probably the only atmosphere in the place as around seventy thousand United fans failed to make any impression at all. Old Trafford seemed like a dismal, dour place. I know they call it the theatre of dreams but the majority of their fans take it far too literally. They clap politely as if they are at the opera. After the break Vidic made it four and it looked like Ferguson's wishes would be granted. The crowd clapped politely. The purple faced Scot showed no respect at all by putting Tevis on to play alongside Rooney, Berbatov and

Ronaldo, he smelled blood and was going for the kill with his full array of striking talent.

The Tigers had other ideas though as we got stuck into them and our task by continuing to press forward through the gaps in midfield. Mendy worked well down the right lobbing the advancing van der Sar as the Dutchman tried to thwart him. Despite a great clearance from Vidic, the ball was clearly over the line and a goal was rightly awarded. Mendy then tormented Ferdinand on the left and forced him to give away a penalty which Geovanni dispatched with consummate ease. At 4-3 Ferguson was now in grave danger of being hoisted by his own petard. He brought on a defender to steady the ship and see out the final few nerve jangling minutes. City players and fans gave it everything they had and only just came up short after being the first team to score three goals at Old Trafford in getting on for a hundred games. We had the champions of Europe rattled and no one more so than Wayne Rooney. The shaven headed striker charged around like a bull in a china shop as he has done countless times before. You can always tell when things aren't going well in Wayne's world, steam starts to come out of his ears as his head comes to the boil. In the end he was lucky to escape a red card and his increasingly desperate quest to claim his hundredth goal would have to go on to the next game. This was one of those bizarre situations when we played so well in defeat that it seemed like a win. If we could play anything like we did in the second half in our upcoming games, then we had every chance of getting back to winning ways and continuing our remarkable start.

George Boateng was interviewed after the game and his comments revealed so much about our mentality at the moment. Of course he was pleased that we had scored three goals at Old Trafford but bitterly disappointed to leave with no points. There was no doubt that we had to put this game behind us and concentrate on the next, just as we had been doing all season. Once clear of Manchester and on the M62 we stopped at a service station to get a drink and something to eat. As we went in Milo spotted a familiar face.

"It's Daniel Cousin," he said in complete surprise. It was and Milo wasted no time in walking up to him and congratulating him on a good game.

"Thanks," he said probably using one of the very few words of English he knows. A blonde fan went across and planted a kiss on Daniel's cheek leaving him bemused and ever so slightly embarrassed as he walked away with his three young children in tow. For the second game in a row I rated Cousin as man of the match amongst so many who played well.

Joanna had to go into hospital on Monday to have an operation on two toes. The result would be that she had to keep her feet up for two weeks. There was no way she was going to miss a game though, so we organised a wheel chair and swapped her pass for disabled tickets at the KC for the Bolton and Manchester City games. Alice gladly agreed to come along as Joanna's carer much to the annoyance of Finn. I think he fancied pushing her around for the day and maybe having a go in the chair himself, although he did lose a bit of interest when I explained it wouldn't be a high tech model like they use in the Olympics. Joanna really was in an awful lot of pain after the operation. She had her big and second toes broken and pinned, it made me squirm just looking at them. Wayne Rooney and David Beckham's famous broken metatarsals had nothing on this, I can assure you. I took the week off work to nurse Joanna and look after the kids. Although it was hard work, I have to say that I quite enjoyed being a house husband. Maybe it wasn't such a bad option after all.

Hull City 0 Bolton Wanderers 1
Saturday 8th November 2008

I picked up the wheelchair on the morning of the game. Once we got the hang of putting it up and adjusting various bits and pieces to get it just right for Joanna, Alice took over as designated driver. The gusto with which she carried out her duties took me by surprise. We also got a rare flash of her humour as she wheeled an increasingly embarrassed Joanna towards the stadium.

"Once I get you in you'll be fine," she said in a stage whisper.

"I'll get you some food and mash it up for you, to make it easier."

Joanna turned crimson as she held her head in her hands. We got Joanna in place at pitch level at the East side of the ground.

"Don't forget if the ball comes to you just head it back," I said reassuringly.

I took the boys to our regular seats just in time for the kick off.

The club had flirted with the idea of applause to commemorate Remembrance Sunday but had decided quite rightly, that the proper convention of silence was the only way to proceed.

I know why they thought about this though. Football fans, especially the beered up variety, find it notoriously difficult to keep quiet but surely for this special day they could manage it.

Clearly not, as it turned out. A small section of Bolton fans thought it highly amusing to go early. Boos rang out around the ground including their own right minded support and the referee correctly blew his whistle well short of a minute to continue with the match. It was all very disappointing; things like this should transcend football rivalries.

Another big contingent of away fans shared the north stand, courtesy again of free coaches from the Bolton chairman. Well you've got to get them in somehow. I wouldn't mind a bit of free travel myself actually. I daren't add up how much we have spent so far or how much the final tab will be. I started to fill in a Premier League survey but I got cold feet when I got to the questions about cost. To be honest, I think it's best that I don't know.

The game had a slightly scrappy quality to it from the off, more like a Championship game than Premier League affair. Bolton are a workmanlike side, not dirty by any means but strong, tough and straight forward. Any flair that we had shown up to now deserted us as we failed to establish a foothold in the game. Passes went astray, possession was given up cheaply and finishing looked hap hazard. It all made for poor viewing for die hard fans let alone the neutral observer. For their part Bolton did what they do best, win ugly. A Matt Taylor goal separated the teams early in the second half and although we threw on Mendy, Folan and Ricketts, in search of goals, we failed to find the net ourselves.

Milo called Joanna straight after the final whistle. He claimed it was a conspiracy, he had it all worked out.

"Phil Brown has done a deal," he said.

"He lets Bolton win and then Bolton's chairman is going to sack Megson and give Brownie the job."

"Milo, you've been drinking again, haven't you?" Joanna asked.

In truth a mixture of poor finishing and outstanding reaction keeping from Jaaskelainen between the Bolton sticks ensured that while it was hell for us, to Hull and back was a pleasurable experience for the Trotters. The Bolton fans celebrated as if they had just won the FA Cup. I think it was more a case of joy unconfined after winning back to back games than the thought of beating the mighty Hull City. I was left thinking that this was surely the type of match made for Dean Windass. Sadly I also tend to think that the manager believes that particular ship may be getting ready to sail. Losing to last seasons two best teams in Europe is one thing but losing at home to Bolton is altogether a different proposition. There was a lot of talk about bubbles bursting now. We needed to get back to winning ways and quickly, otherwise there was a very real danger of a prolonged slump at a time when teams in the bottom half of the table were picking up the pace and points to boot. This season's Premier League campaign was shaping up to be the most open and competitive for many a year.

Hull City 2 Manchester City 2
Sunday 16th November 2008

A four o'clock, Sunday kick off meant that this would be our first live showing on Sky as a Premier League team. We had put to rest the curse of Sky a long time ago, so that didn't worry me. I wasn't particularly worried about Manchester City either. The weight of expectation and Saudi money appeared to be laying heavily on everyone concerned over in the blue half of Manchester. Mark Hughes had already secured the dreaded vote of confidence from his chairman, who was obviously impatient that his recent acquisitions hadn't won the Premier League title yet.

Star man Robinho also seemed disturbed. It was widely reported that he had sacked his agent Wagner Ribeiro. No one is exactly sure why Robinho took this action but I suspect the phone call went a little like this.

"Wagner, Robinho here."

"Robby good to hear from you, how's tricks?"

"Not too clever Waggy to be honest. I thought you said I was signing for a great team from Manchester."

"Yes that's right and that's the deal I got you."

"But I thought you meant United not City."

"Ah, then you should have read the small print Robby,"

"You're fired mate," said Robinho as he slammed the phone down.

"Robby....? Robby....?"

Of course the conversation would have been in Portuguese as the most expensive player in Britain doesn't speak a word of the Queens English. It seems bizarre therefore that Hughes had handed Robinho the captaincy for this game. It could only be to keep him happy but if that's the best the manager can come up with, I don't expect either of them to be at the club that much longer. Manchester City are far from a one man team though and on their day they are capable of giving anyone a game. Stephen Ireland is the pick of the bunch for me. He's a real box to box player who scores great goals. Ireland's career is not without controversy though. He apparently told lies about his grandmother's death to be excused from international duty while Steve Staunton held the reigns of the Irish side. This all came as a great shock to everyone particularly Stephen's granny who was alive and kicking. Rumours have since circulated that the Irishman was upset about receiving dog's abuse in the dressing room over his failed hair transplant. For God's sake Steve, get over it. Being bald is not all that bad, oh apart from the obvious bouncer and Peter Kenyon connections of course.

Joanna still needed a wheelchair for this game. Her foot was healing well but she still had to keep her weight off it as much as possible. Joanna's mother duly obliged as carer for the game. Unfortunately injury elsewhere to Andy Dawson meant that he wouldn't recover in time and we would start with Sam Ricketts as the only change to the side that lost to Bolton a week earlier.

Paul Duffen had urged the Tigers fans to get behind the players and make some noise, in the wake of news that the KC was officially the quietest in the Premier League. I do think it's slightly unfair to give us this tag when we are also one of the smallest capacities in the league. I'd argue that man for man we out sing that rabble at the Old Trafford for example. We should be better though and if we could replicate some of the noise we make away from home then the KC will become a fearsome place for visiting teams.

The fans took notice of the chairman and responded in fine voice, especially when Cousin pounced on a defensive schoolboy error to slide the ball past the advancing Joe Hart. Joanna forgot about her foot for a second and jumped up waving her scarf around her head. Feeling like a charlatan she quickly slid back down into her chair and hoped that nobody had noticed.

The Tigers looked comfortably in control and I was convinced that more goals would surely follow. Cousin turned from hero to villain though as he gave the ball up cheaply in midfield. Robinho gratefully collected the stray pass and then inexplicably passed it into space and not the path of any advancing team mate. Myhill failed to claim the ball and poor Zayette took two errant touches' to gift Stephen Ireland with a goal which was the result of at least three schoolboy errors of our own. The Irishman pounced again later in acres of space, to curl the ball just beyond Myhill's searching finger tips.

As the half drew to a close the complexion of the game had changed completely. We surrendered control and it was the other City who now looked like the better outfit.

My mate Dave came down from his lofty position in the west stand to have a chat.

"I hope the teacups, saucers, spoons and kettle are flying in the changing room," I said, as I failed to suppress my disappointment in any meaningful way.

Whatever the manager did say at the break seemed to work a treat as we looked like a different team in the second half. Geovanni started to prove a point to his former club and put his high cost countryman firmly in his place. His free kick took a wicked deflection past the despairing keeper before nestling in the back of the net to level the scores at two apiece.

Geo then got three chances to win it for us with a free kick on the edge of the area as referee Phil Dowd stuck to the letter of the law enforcing the Manchester players to maintain the regulation ten yards.

"You're the captain Robinho, sort them out," I shouted as the Brazilian stood unwilling or unable to communicate to his team mates while the kick was taken again and again.

"What's the Portuguese for 'what a waste of money'?" I asked the bloke next to me. Myhill pulled off a point blank save from Vassell in the dying seconds and as the whistle went, I think most people were happy with the draw. Honours even then but when it came to the boys from Brazil, there was no doubt that our own player represented much better value for money.

Maradona, the hand balling, drug taking, stomach stapling, Argentinean demigod, was in Scotland for a friendly in his first game in charge of his national side. As he was on British soil, the press naturally wanted to ask about the 'hand of God' goal again. He had the audacity to compare it to Geoff Hurst's goal in 1966, claiming that England cheated. This was music to the ears of the Scots of course. They are only too happy to embrace anyone who has managed to put one over England. It's a, 'My enemy's enemy is my friend' kind of thing and it proves that although there is no doubt that he is a cheat, the loathsome South American is certainly no fool.

I think George Burley's assistant Terry Butcher, showed remarkable composure in not shaking Maradona warmly by the throat after the game. Elsewhere Capello's English revolution rumbled on as the Germans fell to us in Berlin. Our own band of internationals came home unscathed from their matches to ensure that City would be pretty much a full strength outfit for the next game.

Portsmouth 2 Hull City 2
Saturday 22nd November 2008

Our longest League trip of the season required an early start, so having packed the car up the night before we bundled two very tired kids into the back and set off for the south coast on Saturday morning. My mate Dave is starting a new job in Portsmouth after Christmas and he intends to stay in digs during the week and commute at the weekend. He reckons you can do the trip down there in four and a half hours, no problem. Well you can't, not unless Lewis Hamilton is driving, not unless every speed camera on the way is broken and not unless you have a bladder the size of a basketball. It took us five and a half hours including one short pit stop at Watford Gap.

I have been to Portsmouth exactly two times in my life. The first was on a holiday with my mam and dad in 1977. I remember we toured the length of Britain. My dad really must have liked driving because we went up to Loch Lomond and down to Weymouth in one week. While on the south coast we took a short trip to Portsmouth and jumped on the ferry to Cherbourg for my one and only trip to France. All I knew about the French was that they had never forgiven us for Agincourt and could never quite bring themselves to thank us for saving them in two World Wars. That day trip only served to underline those views. We wandered around the town with no sign of 'entant cordial' and had a brief stop for some food before we caught the boat back to England. In comparison to the French, southerners seemed like long lost friends. My only other trip to Nelson's favourite city was earlier this year. I went to visit a company through work. I had a very busy day and got to meet some interesting people including Nigel who was an avid Burnley fan and a woman from Sheffield who was a Blade rather than an Owl. When they found out I was a City supporter she asked me a question. "How do you think you'll do this season?"

I thought for a second and realised that the bitter pain of relegation would still be burning inside of her, especially as West Ham had broken the transfer rules and stayed up at their expense. I decided to be tactful in my answer. I was going to say that it would be tough but we'd give it a go but before I could speak she cut in.

"You'll go down," she declared.

"Well, I don't know, I…."

"No you'll go down, definitely."

How arrogant could you get? I wanted to tell her that she shouldn't tar us with their brush. Sheffield United went down because they played like drains in the second half of the season but I decided that discretion was the better part of valour and refused to bite. I couldn't help thinking though, that she would be the first I'd call to rub her nose in it, if we did manage to stay up.

Fratton Park is best described as 'crumbling splendour.' Built in 1898, I think it still has the original Victorian plumbing.

The sinks in the Gents definitely looked a more inviting option than the grotty urinals. There is a newish stand opposite the away end and at one side the seats are shaded to give a picture of what looks a little like former owner and saviour, Milan Mandoric. To be honest it really could be anyone, it looks like a Rolf Harris painting.

"Can you tell what it is yet?" I said to Joanna.

Although it is the smallest ground in the Premier League, Pompey's support is fanatical and given that our away following is equally vocal, there was a good atmosphere inside the dilapidated stadium.

Portsmouth started by far the better as we struggled to get into any kind of rhythm. The extravagantly named Papa Bouba Diop rattled the crossbar with the ball landing just the right side of the line and spinning out. They continued to pressurise until Peter Crouch rose in the box to plant a simple, unchallenged header into the net. For all his 6ft 7in skeletal frame, Crouch is not that good in the air. He jumps like I imagine a Giraffe would, if it could and by that I mean about six inches off the ground. He seems to rely on the accuracy of the pass as the ball ricochets off his ten bob shaped head. Our cries of, 'Does the circus know you're here?' seemed like water off a giraffes back to the freakish front man, as Portsmouth were good value for their lead. We gradually shaped up though and started to control the game. Geovanni hit the joint of bar and post as he looped a long range effort past the admiring James. At the break Joanna turned to me and whispered,

"Fagan's sat behind me."

I turned round to have a look but couldn't see the injured star.

"Where?" I asked.

"Two rows back," she said.

"Nope, still can't see him."

"There," she said pointing directly at an old bearded man who looked like he had stepped directly off a West End stage.

"Oh….Fagin, as in Oliver," I said.

We sometimes try to spot celebrities at halftime in order to fight off the boredom. Most times they are look-alikes but occasionally they are real. I once spotted comic actor Stephen Frost at the KC and last season I saw Basil Brush's sidekick Roy North at Sellhurst Park. Thankfully Mr. Roy didn't have the rabid fox with him.

We continued to dominate in the second half when the breakthrough came as Turner steeled in at the far post to head in unchallenged. City now looked capable of going on for the win but Glen Johnson had other ideas. He collected a clearance on his chest and swung his wrong foot at the ball to claim what must be goal of the season and also retake the lead. It didn't look like it was going to be our day despite playing very well against a very useful side. We never know when we are beaten though and the introduction of Halmosi, Stelios and the back in favour Windass signalled one last hurrah. It was that man again who got the equaliser as Deano pressured the defender from a corner. Is there anything that Windass can't do? Ironic cheers rang out around the ground but this time it was us doing the singing. He may be a fat, old footballer but let's be honest; he is our fat, old footballer.

We drove up to Bracknell after the game and stopped in one of Lenny Henry's favourite hotels to save us being on the road for close on twelve hours in one day. The next morning it was just a short drive to the village of Bray where we decided to have something to eat before we went home. We went to the Hind's Head, Heston Blumenthal's pub. The food is not experimental or ridiculously expensive, like it is at his famous Fat Duck restaurant. In place of premium priced snail porridge or egg and bacon ice cream, there is the more traditional Sunday roast and treacle tart on offer and I have to say that this was probably the best pub lunch we have ever had. All the travelling and excitement played havoc with Joanna's poor foot over the weekend. It had swelled up like a balloon and it really was giving her gip but she was as keen as me to see every Premier League game this season and she wasn't going to let a gammy foot stop her.

Stoke City 1 Hull City 1
Saturday 29th November 2008

Stoke are Nick Hancock's favourite team. It's good to see a celebrity supporting his home town club rather than one of the glamour teams, as most others seem to do. The former quiz show hosting, actor and comedian took a sabbatical from show business to work for a mate's mortgage company recently. It must be the credit crunch biting lately because I saw him joining Alan Hansen and Lulu in a Morrison's Christmas commercial the other day. Added to this he comes from a town that really can be described as crap. He supports a team that play the worst style of football imaginable alongside the fans with the biggest mouths in the Premier League. Being Nick Hancock can't be that much fun can it?

While I harbour no ill feeling towards Hancock, I can't say the same for Stoke City. Everything from Tony Pulis's baseball cap to Roary Delap's long throw winds me up. Everyone has a team they despise and mine is Stoke, they play anti-football. I was still looking forward to the game though because I thought that Phil Brown, Brian Horton and Steve Parkin could summon up the tactical nous to outsmart the witless Welshman. At least I hoped they would and we could leave Stoke as quickly as possible with all the points.

Joe missed his first game of the season. He had entered a competition with the library services to draw his favourite characters from a book he had read. He chose Tin Tin and Snowy. It turned out that he won the first prize for his age group and the first overall prize. The presentation was due the day of the game so Milo took him to that. Joe is no stranger to winning competitions. Last year he did a sea life painting for a Royal Mail competition during school half term. Joanna encouraged him to do it mainly as a way of beating boredom. It was left in an envelope on the kitchen table for quite a while, in fact it might still have been there but I decided to stick a stamp on it and put it in the post. It was a cracking painting but we never really expected to hear anymore about it to be honest. I mean these type of competitions get thousands of entries don't they? I went to our penultimate game of that season at Cardiff with Tiger Travel. It was a game we really needed to win in order to stay in the Championship. We'd just left the service station after a short stop when my mobile rang.

"Pete you'll never guess what has happened," Joanna shouted down the phone. My mind started racing. What was the problem? Had there been an accident? Was anyone hurt?

I couldn't understand her, she was shouting and babbling at the same time.

"Joanna calm down and tell me slowly, what's happened?"

"Joe has won first prize in the drawing competition."

"Oh, wow that's great, what has he won?"

"A two week family holiday in Florida, all in."

"What! You're joking, really, that's unbelievable." Now it was my turn to shout and babble.

When I got off the phone I couldn't wipe the smile off my face. As we approached Ninian Park the sun was shinning, Joe had just won the prize of a lifetime and City were about to play one of the most important games in their history. How could we fail now? Of course we didn't fail and that man Windass scored the goal to virtually ensure we maintained our Championship status. The rest is history as they say.

Rather than waste Joe's ticket, Joanna invited her mother along to Stoke. Since she came to the Man City game Denise has been dying to go again. She was very excited at the prospect of her first ever away match. I was a little worried about the bad language, not mine or other fans though. Denise has been known to swear like a drunken docker with Tourette's on the odd occasion. It was freezing cold down at Stoke. The Britannia Stadium is fairly new but it looks as if it was designed by David Blunkett. There is no real symmetry to the ground and it has two open corners which allow the inclement weather straight through. Fog swept down across the pitch periodically. It looked a little bit like smoke crossing a battlefield in a scene from a film about the battle of Waterloo, maybe a pointer for the afternoon to come. We certainly felt as though we were in a battle as The Potters launched an aerial bombardment probably not seen since 1815. Long ball followed long throw all game long as Stoke played the only way they know how. They were ably assisted by a Napoleon like figure in the middle. Keith Stroud has both the stature and the manner of the mercurial Frenchman and he wasted no time showing his colours by allowing Stoke's bully boy tactics to prosper. We tried to play good football in the manner it is intended, you know to feet on the deck and that sort of thing. We got our just reward with an extremely well taken effort from Marlon King on the stroke of halftime.

Throughout the game we coped very well with Stoke's route one game. Rory Delap's long throw didn't cause us many problems, mainly because we have two very strong centre backs who have no trouble heading the ball. Dean Windass employed a tactic of warming up next to Delap whenever he lined up to throw at that side of the pitch. It only seemed to amuse Delap but to be honest I'd have thought that the sight of the burly front man stretching and lunging would be enough to put anyone off their stroke. Deano was also willing to take one for the team as Napoleon issued him a yellow card for unsporting behaviour after he persisted to worry Delap. Ricketts and McShane did their bit as well by using the same towels that Rory had strategically placed around the pitch for his own throws, much to the annoyance of Pulis and his fans. Stoke have the reputation for being the loudest in the Premier League. It's a claim I can't argue with and when they launch into their version of Delilah, it sounds very much like a battle cry. They have obviously never heard the Tom Jones classic though because although they clearly knew the words, there was no discernable tune at all. Our own fans were in fine voice again and sensed that the Tigers were comfortable in this game. I couldn't see Stoke getting back into it really.

Simonson launched yet another high bomb from defence and as it came down with snow on it Fuller chased it into the penalty area. The striker went down in instalments as he brushed past the grasping Myhill. There was absolutely minimal contact but if a goalkeeper goes to ground in the box then most experienced forwards will tend to make a meal of it, just ask Deano. Boaz almost atoned for his mistake by getting his hands to Fuller's spot kick but he couldn't quite keep it out and Stoke had a share of the points. It was disappointing but at least it was a point. On the bright side we had coped with Stoke's one and only tactic and we wouldn't have to go to the Britannia in the league for at least another season. Visits to Stoke are definitely occasions when you can justifiably say that the best thing about the place is the road out. You can be on your way and out in probably the quickest time anywhere in the Premier League and that's a real bonus.

After the weekends results and heading into December City were stilled nicely placed in sixth. If anyone had offered us that at the start of the season then hands would have been well and truly bitten off. No team with 22 points or more at the end of December has ever slipped out of the Premier League. We were standing on 23 already with still 15 more up for grabs before 'Old Father Time' had his say. Nobody was counting their chickens, or turkeys but we would have to break yet another record to fail this season. At work I got talking to an Aston Villa fan about City's great start. He agreed we had done exceptionally well and then reverted to the usual football snobbery and predicted that we would fail in the end.

"You might just manage to stay up this season but then at some point you'll do a wedding," he said.

"What?"

"You'll end up just like wedding."

"Oh, right," I said realising that he had something in common with Jonathan Ross. Not only was the guy a Villa fan but he clearly didn't know his R's from his elbow when it came to us.

Hull City 2 Middlesbrough 1
Saturday 6th December 2008

Dave took some of us out for a curry for his leaving do.

Phil was his usual annoying self, trying and sometimes succeeding to wind me up with his customary Chelsea related banter. Luckily the one thing he likes to do more than irritate me is eat mountains of food and the fact that he kept stuffing his face meant he couldn't talk for much of the evening. Wes, another of Dave's workmates, turned up in a very loud red shirt. Actually it was so loud and so red it almost made my eyes water. It was also almost identical to those worn by the waiters, this combined with the fact that Wes is a Brummie of West Indian decent meant that....Well I'm sure you can see where this is going. I looked up every time Wes went to the toilet, expecting to hear someone at one of the other tables shout out to him.

"Two more Lamb Bhuna's over here mate."

Thankfully it never happened. The whole evening was very enjoyable and a fitting send off for Dave but I couldn't help feeling a little bit down as I walked home afterwards. I realised that whether we like it or not all things must pass.

With Roy Keane doing the inevitable and walking away from his ailing Sunderland side, the media focused on Phil Brown as a potential successor. It was obvious if not completely lazy journalism to connect Phil with the Mackems.

He is a South Shields lad and boyhood Black Cat fan. Added to this he is doing pretty well with City at the moment.

Actually he has done extremely well. Two seasons ago we looked like we were going out of the Championship when he took over. Under his leadership we have climbed up to the higher reaches of the Premier League and we have done it by playing decent, attractive football. We have a team capable of holding its own and there are plans in place to improve further and create the really big club that Hull and East Yorkshire have long been waiting for. There is a real expectation that something very important is happening here. In a sense it's a potential fairytale and unless I missed my guess, you don't walk away from a fairytale, especially into a bit of a horror story up on Wearside.

Middlesbrough came to town on the back of a reasonable run in the league. They are a strange side, on their day they can either beat or lose to anyone. Obviously I was hoping for the latter. The game was best described as scrappy and although Middlesbrough looked to have slightly the better of the opening exchanges, quality was lacking on both sides. Passes went astray often and possession was given up far too easily for my liking. Geovanni revealed that the one chink in his armour was his heading ability, as he steered successive sitters towards opposite corner flags.

"For God's sake use your feet," I shouted.

As the game wore on, I got the feeling that one goal would clinch it. As so often happens in games, a questionable refereeing decision in the Middlesbrough half lead to a counter attack and a relatively easy tap in for Tuncay late on.

I honestly thought that was it but these City players really don't ever give up. Halmosi and Mendy had given us extra width and more emphasis in attack and it was the Frenchman whose searching run down the right resulted in a rasping shot. The ball rebounded off the post and hit the unfortunate keeper on the back to cross the line. The Tigers smelled blood and went for the kill. Geovanni collected the ball in the Boro half and headed for goal. Wheater did what Myhill had done a week earlier in allowing the striker the opportunity to claim a penalty. The talented Brazilian duly obliged and as the last man, the unfortunate Wheater saw red and left the field. Geo looked very disappointed that after doing the hard part, King took the ball and the spot kick from him. There were no hard feelings though as he stroked the ball home to claim the unlikely win. Poor Gareth Southgate had an extremely long face at the post match interview as he bemoaned his side's misfortune. The Tigers had snatched victory from the jaws of defeat and ended a run of six matches without a win.

I took Finn and some of his friend's paintballing the day after the game as a belated treat for his birthday. I decided not to take part myself. The idea of running around the woods on a freezing December morning and getting pinged by paintballs with the velocity of flying marbles is not my idea of fun these days. A much better idea was to foot the bill for the youngsters and let them get on with it. I preferred to sit in a warm car with a flask of hot tea and the radio tuned into Talksport.

Milo also came along to the event, with a couple of his friends. I think the idea was to teach the younger upstarts a bit of a lesson but he obviously forgot how devious and cunning fifteen year olds can be. Finn's team came out on top and he wasted no time exercising bragging rights with Milo as the war stories came thick and fast on the way home.

Liverpool 2 Hull City 2
Saturday 13th December 2008

Inevitably there was a lot of disappointment in the run up to this game. With the ticket applications being massively oversubscribed, a lot of people were always going to miss out. It's certainly the one away fixture that stood out for me at the start of the season and I was very relieved to have secured a ticket for the game. It didn't seem right to me that one or two people sported Liverpool scarves in our end and had therefore taken tickets away from genuine City fans. Surely a loyalty scheme rather than an open ballot would be the better option where away tickets are hard to come by.

I have been to Liverpool many times. It's a city that has a special place in my heart. It has a lot in common with Hull; both places are major ports with down to earth, working class communities. In addition to being the home of the team I had a brief dalliance with in 1971, Liverpool is also the home of the Beatles, another of the great loves of my life. I've only been to Anfield once before and not to watch football. We went last summer to see Paul McCartney play as part of the City of culture events. We ended up high in the Centenary stand with the Kop to our left. We were sat next to a genuine Scouser who turned out to be a Liverpool fan as well. I got chatting to him and found that we had something in common. One of his two great heroes was John Lennon, I couldn't disagree with his choice there. The other one was Kenny Dalglish, as I say; John Lennon was one of my heroes too. The Liverpool fan knew all about City and seemed genuinely pleased that we had made it to the top flight at last. He was less happy about McCartney as he moaned almost constantly and complained that the singer's voice had gone. This, of course is the musical equivalent of a footballers legs going. I actually thought Macca was pretty good. He did almost all of his hits and covered Lennon and

George Harrison songs as well. This delighted the big crowd, especially Yoko Ono and Olivia Harrison who where sat in the expensive seats rattling their jewellery. The former Beatle also did a couple of obligatory songs from his latest album to help boost sales. Picking up a mandolin seemed to be the last straw for my new Scouse mate.

"For God's sake, John Lennon must be turning in his grave."

Marlon King made the tabloids during the week leading up to the Liverpool match, courtesy of a visit to a trendy West End club. It was alleged that he assaulted a girl. I believe that everyone is innocent until proven guilty but this incident followed on from a previous one, when he had a scuffle with Dean Windass. This surely indicates that Marlon would be better served by giving the clubs a wide berth for a bit. In any event the manager is standing by the player while the investigation runs its course and he was included in the squad against Liverpool.

Although tickets for the match were like gold dust, Milo managed to get a ticket for the corporate seats. It's a long story but just let's say that Milo knows someone, who knows someone, who knows Alan Hansen.

"If you see Hansen, tell him he's an idiot will you?" I said.

"You'd better wait until after the match though."

Milo went into the Arkles for a pre match nerve settler. He must have felt a little bit isolated because he ordered a drink using his best Scouse accent.

"A pint of lager and a cheeky Vimto please luv," he said sounding like a cross between Steven Gerrard and Dale Winton.

"We don't sell cheeky Vimto's la," said the less than impressed barmaid.

"What part of Scotland are you from anyway?"

"Ok, fair enough just the lager then," said the freshly outed Yorkshire man. While Milo enjoyed prawn sandwiches with the enemy, we sat with the real fans in the Anfield Road end. The atmosphere in the build up to kick off was amazing.

When the Kop sang 'You'll Never Walk Alone," the hairs on the back of my neck stood up and I had to fight the urge to join in. It's no wonder people say that a lot of teams are beaten before they even kick a ball at Anfield.

Liverpool started predictably well, retaining possession for long periods with Gerrard typically involved in everything. We started to play a little ourselves though, with the re-introduced Mendy particularly lively on the right. In fact he gave fullback Dossena a torrid time. Mascherano handled in the area but the referee refused to give us a penalty in what proved to be the first of three big decisions he got wrong on the day. Mendy won a foul on the right flank, the rebound from the resultant free kick was picked up by Marlon King and floated back to the far post. McShane rose above the defence to claim his first goal in black and amber.

Our fans went wild and rightly so but when Mendy continued to beast the Liverpool defence we went in to a fantasy world as Carragher turned the ball past Reina for a two goal deficit.

Everyone was in dreamland now. We actually were Mauling the mighty Reds. Sadly, it wasn't to last. The man who makes Liverpool tick got them level with two neat strikes despite Alan Wiley and his assistant missing successive fouls on Turner, which should have ruled both of Gerrard's goals out. Naturally we felt aggrieved about the poor decisions but how far have we come, to be disappointed with only a 2-2 draw at Anfield?

Outside the ground partially stunned and slightly relieved Scousers offered their opinions. Almost all agreed that we had taken the game to Liverpool and deserved not only to get something from the game but also had earned the right to be playing in the same league. It was genuine praise and very welcome.

Hull City 1 Sunderland 4
Saturday 20th December 2008

Sunderland had registered an excellent win over West Brom in the game before this one, so their spirits were high.

It seems as if the monkey that was Roy Keane could be off the player's backs. Caretaker manager Ricky Spragia looks to be universally liked by the players. So despite the fact that we were favourites for the win, this had all the makings of a banana skin game.

Another record crowd nudged the stadium towards capacity as both home and away supporters tried to get into the Christmas spirit. To be fair the Sunderland fans seemed to be enjoying themselves more than us. I suppose an away day from Sunderland is enough reason to be cheerful at any time of the year, even if the destination is Hull.

The man in charge for this game was none other than Mike Riley, or 'Earthworm Jim' as Finn likes to call him.

He is without a shadow of a doubt the worst referee on the Premier League circuit. The omens were not good for this game. Yet again we went behind to an early goal as Steed Malbranque took advantage of some particularly slack marking to produce an excellent finish.

We got back on level terms when Nicky Barmby rolled back the years with his own consummate footwork.

The second half was end to end with both sides seeming to sacrifice quality in midfield in favour of getting in to the opposition box. Cousin showed some neat play only to find his goal ruled out for a slight offside. The game appeared to be heading for a draw when a speculative shot from Richardson took a wicked deflection off Zayette and wrong footed Myhill. The goal seemed to take most of the wind out of us and when Riley dismissed Ricketts for a second bookable offence, we deflated fully and the game was all but over.

We tried to reorganise but chasing the game with ten men is always an extremely difficult proposition. The task was made harder by the fact that Sunderland were able to catch us on the break with their pace and quality up front. Kenwin Jones and Cisse both netted as Sunderland managed to grab themselves a very flattering win.

I don't actually think that we were that bad but it just shows how cruel and unforgiving this Premier League is sometimes. We had an early taste of how hard it can be against Wigan and now we had just had a repeat dose with the Black Cats.

After the final whistle I reflected on just how much I hate losing. There is nothing worse than witnessing opposing players and fans celebrating and the Mackems got into the party spirit with relish. It just made my day even worse.

It's clear that our home form is nowhere near as good as our away performances. The main reason for this must be the way we set up to play. While a counter attacking style suits us away from the KC, it can't be a benefit at home facing teams who employ the same tactic. Mr. Brown and his team need to put their thinking caps on and come up with a cunning plan and pretty soon.

I was certainly in no mood to do the Christmas shopping. As usual we left it as late as possible. I'm definitely not one of those who has everything wrapped up by September. People may be struggling to pay the bills but there was no holding back on Christmas. It looked just as busy as ever to me. There didn't seem much festive spirit around with impatient shoppers barging into people and grumpily going about their business. It's getting more and more desperate as the years go by.

Wayne Rooney's wife Coleen showed no awareness of the credit crunch or the impact that it is having on ordinary people. She wrote in her magazine column that Wayne had splashed out on a new Baby Bentley for her. Stunning proof, that she knows the price of everything and the value of nothing.

Manchester City 5 Hull City 1
Friday 26th December 2008

Christmas cheer was decidedly thin on the ground as we went into the game that would mark the half way point of the season. The Tigers seem to have hit a rough patch and my own spirits were lower than a snake's belly. It's not that I dislike Christmas or anything, it's just that it has become a particularly melancholy time for me. New Year is little better in my eyes. Why celebrate another year over and another one less to do? I did my best for the kids but it was difficult not to slip into a morose, maudlin, malady. Why do most of the words associated with misery start with the letter 'm'? Apparently these feelings are common to men in their forties. Maybe that's why many have a mid life crisis. They often start buying motorbikes, wear leather trousers, dye their hair and flirt with younger women. My only flirtation is with Hull City and while it is an obsession I don't really think it's a problem.

I couldn't rely on the football to take my mind off things. To be absolutely honest, City had started to look a bit ropey lately and I didn't have a lot of confidence for this match. Still, crossing the Pennines gave us a chance to visit a new ground and for Joe to see his cousins in Manchester.

The City of Manchester stadium or 'Eastlands' as it is more commonly known, is an impressive place. Built originally for the Commonwealth games it was then handed over for City to use rather than let it stand idle. The famous 'B of the bang' sculpture stands outside the ground. The tribute to Linford Christie's comment about starting a race at the 'B' of the starting pistol bang, looks like a huge rusty tropical plant. Apparently it has actually corroded to a hazardous degree and it is due to be removed, hopefully before any of the spikes fall off and skewer fans like human kebabs. I expected to see a running track around the pitch but that has gone, I assume in favour of a wider playing surface. As opposed to their near neighbours in the red half of Manchester, the average City crowd is reckoned to be made up of genuine Mancs. I found I couldn't disagree as I appeared to see extras from 'Shameless,' everywhere I looked inside the ground. While things were a bit hit and miss at home, our away form was decidedly better having lost only once all season. Injuries and suspensions forced Phil Brown into some drastic changes for this game. Mendy reverted to right back, McShane switched to the left and Windass started his first Premier League game for us. Amidst these changes we maintained our attacking four, three, three formation. Unfortunately for us the approach turned out to be utterly cavalier as we allowed enough space behind the fullbacks for a jumbo jet to land let alone be exploited by the twin creative threat of Ireland and Robinho. We succumbed to wave after wave of sky blue attacks as our defence looked about as solid as a MFI wardrobe. We were down by four at the break by virtue of a Caciedo and Robinho brace each.

It was difficult to raise a smile but the fans around us did their best to lift our spirits. There is a small group of supporters who we sit near at away games. As well as getting right behind the team, they are always intent on having a good laugh and this match was no different. Ably directed by a lad Joanna has described as 'Peter Kay's brother,' they ripped mercilessly into an opposing fan who was wearing a ludicrously large baseball cap. After about twenty minutes of abuse he couldn't take any more and he removed the cap. Sadly for him, this only made matters worse. He revealed himself to be ginger and Peter Kay's brother started up all over again.

Phil Brown brought the players over to us at halftime, I thought to applaud the crowd and apologise for such a poor performance. He sat them all down on the pitch though and delivered his team talk there and then. Only the teams reaction in the second half and the next few matches would dictate if this was a good move or not. At any rate something had to change for the second half or we could be into double figures. Windass was sacrificed and pulled off at halftime. This must have come as a big shock to Deano as he normally just got a cup of tea and a Jaffa Cake. To be fair we did improve in the second half but the game was over as a spectacle and we were just playing for pride. The only plus point was the return of Craig Fagan who scored just before Stephen Ireland's richly deserved strike finished the rout. It's a funny thing but even after the worst display of the season so far, my own personal gloom started to lift. We went on to Pam and Alex's for some Boxing Day cheer and were greeted by the site of a huge poster showing Joe's cousin Charlie wearing an oxygen mask. Charlie was chosen by a family friend to be the face of the yes vote for the Manchester congestion charge. Unfortunately the 'clean air for the sake of the children' argument failed to cut any ice with the petrol heads. Jeremy Clarkson devotees said no in droves.

Media luvvie and self confessed Gooner Piers Morgan did a very good article in the Mail on Sunday. He had asked the readers to vote for their football personality of the year and a resounding 44% of the votes went to our very own Captain Fantastic, with David Beckham lagging amongst the also ran's in single figures. Morgan proclaimed Ash as a true life hero who has battled against a career threatening injury and led his team through all divisions. Comparisons were drawn with David Beckham. Who can forget 'Golden Ball's' own battle with injury when he heroically overcame a broken metatarsal? He has also now reached his own career zenith as he's become the unofficial shirt salesman for LA Galaxy and AC Milan. Morgan will present the City captain with a cheque for his chosen charity early in the New Year. It always seemed to me that old Piers was a little bit up himself but my opinion of him has changed. Certainly when it comes to football, the man knows his onions.

Halftime

I have seen my share of halftime entertainment over the years, recent events in Manchester not withstanding. Penalty shoot outs, crossbar challenges, mascot races, jugglers, marching bands, cheer leaders, majorettes....The list is endless.

I seem to remember a Stetson wearing Don Robinson riding around Boothferry Park on a horse and I think we even had a dancing bear during his tenure at some point. One of my recent favourites at the KC has been the Royal Marine Commando display team. Roary get's amongst them and gives them a good old fashioned pasting, only it's not really Roary but a Commando in disguise. The kids love it and so do I.

One of the strangest ones this season was at Blackburn. They had organised a penalty shoot out between rival supporters from shirt sponsors, Crown paints factories in Hull and Blackburn. Dermot Gallagher was officiating but instead of his referee kit he sported a long white coat. I can only think he has turned his hand to becoming a fishmonger after his retirement from the game. To ward off boredom you could even try to spot celebrities or their look-alikes, or just read the match programme.

In the absence of any of the above here, I present a selection of photographs from the season. While you're looking at them why not try a little music? Get a comb and some paper. I find that a sheet of Izal toilet roll works best. While it's neither comfortable nor efficient enough for its intended purpose, there is no denying that it has amazing musical properties. Place the paper over the comb. Put the comb up to your pursed lips and make a slight blow come buzz type of noise. You'll find the result staggering. With a grasp of some very basic tunes and a little practice you will sound every bit as good as any majorette with a professional kazoo. I recommend 'Abide With Me,' It's a football classic.

Where the balloon went up and it all kicked off.

Captain Fantastic and Milo.

We were robbed.

Finn and Joe ready to Rock the Casbah.

Crowd control it's the future, I've seen it.

'B' of the bang, 'R' of the rubbish.

On a clear day you can see all the way to Ryan France

Beckham's metatarsal has nothing on this baby

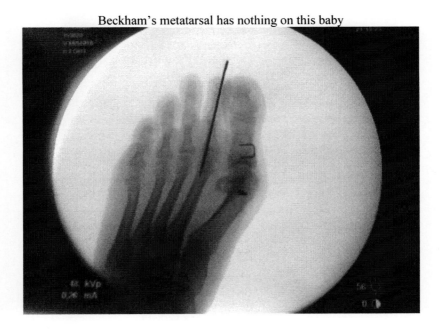

The Duff blimp, sorry Sky camera.

Joe demonstrating the perfect nutmeg.

Brian misplaced the changing room key.

The Cottage where Cottagers….Support their team.

Dave, Jamie and Jonathan put on a brave face.

Alice and Joanna very merry at Bolton.

Patrick and Manucho.

They think it's all over, actually it's only really just begun.

The Second Half

Hull City 0 Aston Villa 1
Tuesday 30th December 2008

Phil Brown had promised changes and he was as good as his word. Out went Boateng and Marney and the four, three, three formation and in came Garcia and Halmosi in a more defensive four, five, one line up. Manchester City and Villa are the two teams I feared the most this season. On their day, Boxing Day for example, both sides are very capable of giving their opponents a hiding but we seemed to have the measure of the Villa.

It was altogether a much better performance with everyone appearing to react well to the manager's public dressing down.

The new system looked to be working well. Aston Villa may have had a bit of an off day and been slightly below par but City deserved great credit for stifling them and looking the more likely to emerge with the win as the game went on.

Rejuvenated Nicky Barmby challenged Freidal in the Villa goal and stabbed home the goalkeeper's fumble.

Referee Steve Bennett ruled the goal out for a foul on Friedal but the replay showed that there was no such infringement and the goal should have stood. In all honesty if the gargantuan goalkeeper had lost the ball to the diminutive City man, then he deserved to concede a goal in my book.

We looked to be heading for a goalless draw as chances at either end were at a premium. City looked a much tighter, well balanced unit and they seemed more like the top four side than Villa. We coped with the pace and guile of Agbonlahor and Young very comfortably and it looked like the only way we could lose was by virtue of a mistake. So it proved to be. Ricketts jumped in to the tackle and missed when Young skipped by him on our left to put over a fizzing cross. The desperately unlucky Zayette increased his own goal tally by getting a thick edge on the ball and managing to steer it past Myhill rather than to safety as he'd intended. All of a sudden we were trailing. In the dying minutes Boaz Myhill came forward for a corner with one last throw of the dice. In the melee and confusion almost all of us saw the ball flicking off the outstretched hand of Ashley Young on the goal line and over the bar. The referee must have seen it as well because he immediately pointed to the spot.

The linesman took up his position at the by-line and Marlon King held the ball waiting to rescue a well deserved point.

What happened next was hard to take. Under pressure from the Villa players and seemingly in contact with someone off the field, Bennett consulted the linesman before changing his mind and awarding a goal kick. After the match and with the benefit of several slow motion replays everyone could see that although the intent was there, Young didn't handle the ball. There was no doubt that the decision was right in the end but the question was, how did the officials reach that decision?

Video replays and advice from the fourth official are not supposed to be used in decisions relating to penalties and if they were used, why didn't they consult on our incorrectly disallowed first half goal? If it wasn't for bad luck, we'd have no luck at all at the moment and the officials seem to have turned against us now as well. On the up side we looked a lot more solid, we did a reasonable job on a good top six team and if we had just got the rub of the green, we could have taken a share of the spoils at the very least.

A home 3rd round FA Cup tie with Newcastle beckoned next. This would be a welcome break and distraction from an increasingly tense Premier League campaign and also a chance to blood some of the fringe players. The pressure was off to an extent because despite what Phil Brown said about wanting a good cup run, the priority really was the League.

Hull City 0 Newcastle 0
FA Cup 3rd round Saturday 3rd January 2009

Phil Brown rang the changes once again for this cup match, seven to be exact. Several key players were rested while Stelios would make his first start in black and amber. Craig Fagan would also make his first start since the horrific injury he suffered at the hands of Danny Guthrie at Newcastle earlier in the season. Our supporters gave Guthrie the kind of reception his cowardly attack deserved. To counter our boos and jeers the Newcastle faithful cheered Danny boy, saying much about their mentality I think. The new line up acquitted themselves well and looked far from a second string outfit.

Newcastle caretaker manager Joe Kinnear had tried to pull a fast one claiming only to have eleven fit players for the game. In truth he fielded his strongest possible side with quality on the bench as well. The match was pretty even with both sides certainly going for a win. Our problems with match officials continued as Chris Foy seemed intent on booking the entire side for relatively innocuous challenges. Michael Owen showed that Capello is no mug by wasting a couple of good chances and perhaps proving that his international career is all but over. Annoyingly Guthrie had a good game and there was certainly no fireworks between him and Fagan. We probably had the best of the chances and definitely made Man City transfer target Shay Given earn his pay. For the second game in a row we were convinced that we had scored as Given seemed to have caught the ball over his line before springing out and wagging his finger at the linesman. It probably was too close to call but it just shows that we desperately need a break at the moment. Newcastle introduced Guteirrez who proceeded to take on and beat McShane for fun at every turn but there was never any final product and the game faded into a predictable draw. A clean sheet is always welcome but nobody really wanted it to go to another game. A long trip north on a cold January evening was not exactly a prospect I relished but news that a victory in the replay would mean a home tie against Millwall or Crewe seemed to cheer up everyone. Who knows, maybe we could progress through the rounds and make a swift return to Wembley. Given the unbelievable events of 2008, I wouldn't rule it out. I'd better get on and book the hotel, just in case.

With the opening of the transfer window came the rumours about our transfer targets and dealings, some were plausible and others just downright ridiculous. While I could see Michael Chopra striding out at the KC for example, I couldn't really imagine Michael Owen shopping in St Stephens Square.

In addition to new players coming in, inevitably old players will be leaving. It looks as though Dean Windass may have finally played his last competitive game for the Tigers. The club released news that they had told Deano that he was free to leave. Ironically it was Brian Horton who got to deliver the message that Deano was not wanted for the second time. It's a real shame because he still had a lot to offer, especially in terms of the experience he could pass on to our younger players. He has been very vocal about wanting to play and it doesn't look like he would get much of a chance here, so a move is probably the best bet for the old stager. He will always hold a special place in Tigers legend as a great servant and the man who scored the goal that got us to the Promised Land.

Everton 2 Hull City 0
Saturday 10th January 2009

Yet another trip to the north west for a game this season and with trips to Wigan and Bolton to come we aren't done yet.
I have to say I'm getting sick to the back teeth of the M62.
We decided to drive across on Friday dropping Joe at his cousin's in Manchester on the way for a sleepover and picking Alice up at the same time for the game. We stayed in Liverpool in a hotel on Albert Dock right opposite the very impressive and fairly newly built Liverpool Echo Arena. Millions of pounds have been pumped into rebuilding and regenerating the city. There was no doubting the positive effect that being the 2008 European city of culture has had on Liverpool. Saturday marked the transition to Vilnius and Linz for 2009, so there was due to be a huge firework celebration on the waterfront that evening, we thought about staying on for that.
Outside of the city centre towards Goodison Park you'll find the badlands that any major city suffers from. In this respect Hull ends up being no different from and in some cases a good deal better than Liverpool, Manchester, Sheffield, Leeds and the like. The thing that sets Liverpool apart though is the people and that unquenchable spirit marked by their sense of humour.
Scousers will make a joke about anything and are not afraid to laugh at themselves. We went into Weatherspoons before the game. It was packed as they usually are on match days and although we found a table to stand our drinks on, we were short of two chairs. Alice spotted a couple leaving so she went across to their table.
"You don't mind if we pinch your chairs do you?"
The two Evertonian's looked up and replied smartly.
"You can pinch anything you like love, you're in Liverpool."

To a lesser degree Everton fans are like Manchester City to United in as much as true locals support the blues. The joke is that most of the Liverpool support comes from North Wales and Scandinavia. The atmosphere inside Goodison was pretty good. In the build up to kick off a young girl walked around the pitch in period costume chucking Everton mints into the crowd, nice touch that. The teams marched out to the theme from 'Z Cars.' The tune came from a traditional folk song called 'Johnny Todd.' Apparently the children of Merseyside used to sing the song, so for that reason it makes sense that Everton adopted it as there own, although Watford use it as well for some reason.

Phil Brown kept the same formation that so nearly paid off against Villa to maintain our 'win ugly' philosophy. Nicky Barmby took the brunt of the home crowd's anger. Having spent four years with Everton he committed the cardinal sin of taking the short trip across Stanley Park to join the Red's earlier in his career. The usually jovial Scousers have never been able to see the funny side of this and don't attempt to disguise their hatred of the Hull man. They sing a very catchy 'Die, Die, Nicky, Nicky, Die.'

Just like the Villa game the plan seemed to be to let Everton have plenty of possession in their own half but not where they could do any harm. Unfortunately we didn't play as well as in that game and as opposed to Villa, Everton's midfield got hold of the ball and actually did things with it. Makeshift strikers Cahill and Fellaini caused us problems with their craft and guile. Even though he was at least a yard offside the Belgian who shares an uncanny resemblance with 'Screech' from 'Saved by the Bell,' nodded home a simple cross to take the lead. King toiled tirelessly as the lone front man but with Brown's plan in tatters by virtue of a goal which should not have stood, we would have to change our formation. Cahill continued to torment us when he won a dubious free kick about thirty yards out on the stroke of halftime. If we could hold out for the whistle then Phil Brown could reform and regroup the troops for the second half and we could possibly get something from the game. Unfortunately Arteta had different ideas when he fired a thunderbolt free kick into the only place where Myhill couldn't get it. That was basically game set and match as far as this match was concerned. We tried going four, four, two in the second half but it was too little, too late. We rarely troubled Howard in the Everton goal and in truth Everton rarely troubled us again. Fellaini picked up the booking that would mean he missed the next two games and to be honest he was lucky to get only that. His liberal use of the elbow against Zayette and Turner in the first half was probably deserving of a red card. Zayette also picked up a booking, meaning he misses the Arsenal match. Our last chance to salvage something from the game came as Halmosi got himself into a good position for once only to see his cross sail high over everyone and into the stand. Honestly, my granny could have done better than that, you'll remember her from the Wigan game. She was very much a utility player my granny, defence, wing play, she could do it all. Walking away from the ground after the game I overheard a telling comment from an Everton fan.

"You can tell Brown learned his trade at Bolton," he said.

I don't think it was meant to be a complement but more a critical assessment of how we have abandoned our attacking style of earlier in the season.

Phil Brown thinks we lack guile, we are too nice. I agree wholeheartedly. What we need is a player who knows how to win fouls and play the game the modern way, a player like Dean Windass. Unfortunately in the same direction our season appears to be going, Deano is also heading west, to Oldham on loan. New faces and fresh blood were needed now more than ever to help halt the slide.

We were in no mood to stay for the firework display that was for sure. We stopped for a quick cuppa in Manchester, picked up Joe and headed home as fast as we could.

The jug eared, crisp munching presenter of Match of the Day was in his element. Our slump in form seemed to cheer him more than a free packet of cheese and onion. He talked of reality checks and sinking stones. His dislike of Hull has been evident since day one of the season and I can only think that someone here owes him money or something.

Maybe he is among the many journalists who have recently lumped on us going down at 40-1. With 40 points probably being the safety mark, they are asking where are the remaining 13 points coming from? It's a fair question but I would ask where are Newcastle and the like going to get their 20 points from? A couple of my mates, Gary and Tony had a bet at the start of the season that City would win the League with a 53 point start at 18-1. They are already on 80 points so there is still more than enough available. I'd love to see them cash in and prove the so called experts wrong.

Newcastle 0 Hull City 1
FA Cup 3rd round replay Wednesday 14th January 2009

We now appeared to be entering the difficult part of the rollercoaster ride, the bit where your heart, stomach and everything else is in your mouth.

What we needed to settle the nerves was a win and we needed it pretty damn quick. To my way of thinking Phil Brown had to put out his strongest team for this one, simply to try and restore some confidence. He obviously didn't see it my way and ended up making eight changes. While you couldn't call it the reserves it was certainly second string. We drove up to Newcastle and we found parking a lot easier without the Saturday shoppers. We faced another long climb to our seats up in the gods at St James' Park. I certainly wasn't expecting to have to do that again this season. This time we were even higher up and the players looked even smaller but we certainly had a bird's eye view of the proceedings.

The first half passed without too much incident. Despite the changes we had a good shape about us and although a full strength Newcastle looked slightly the better side, we were never outclassed. The game didn't really have the feeling of a cup encounter and it all seemed a little bit tame, until Brown and Kinnear squared up that is. Phil took exception to the Newcastle defenders hacking at Cousin and big Joe took exception to Phil.

'Brownie, Brownie knock him out,' resonated from the upper reaches of the away section as the two men stood toe to toe in the technical area. The inevitable result was that referee Dowd sent both managers to the stands. An alarm must have gone off down at FA headquarters, signalling time for them to put away the dominoes and reach for the disciplinary guidelines.

The second half livened up a bit and both sides certainly had a go. Owen looked the most likely or should I say unlikely to score but we dug deep and kept going. Our industry was finally rewarded late on when Mendy went on one of his surging runs and squared the ball into the Newcastle box. Cousin gratefully picked up the resultant pass from Garcia and slotted the ball home for the lead. Newcastle huffed and puffed but never really looked like breaking us down. Caleb Folan made a welcome return from injury and saw out the final few minutes in place of Cousin. We had made it past the 3rd round for the first time in twenty years and a home tie with Millwall would be our reward. Much more importantly we had restored some squad confidence by gaining that all important win. It wasn't all good news for us though. George Boateng picked up a nasty looking injury after playing very well and it turned out to be Paul McShane's last game for us as Sunderland recalled him from his loan. On the transfer front we had inevitably been linked with a whole host of players. Wigan's left winger Kevin Kilbane was signed up quickly and we also managed to snap up Manucho from Man Utd on a season long loan. The tall, rangy Angolan could be an astute acquisition and if he can replicate what Campbell did for us, everyone will be happy.

Hull City 1 Arsenal 3
Saturday 17th January 2009

The win at Newcastle was very welcome but we now had the difficult task of winning in the League. Arsenal would be very hard to beat. They may not be at their best this year but they are still packed full of quality and on their day capable of dispatching any team. They probably also wanted revenge for their embarrassing defeat to us earlier in the season.

Phil Brown was forced to make changes in defence. Ricketts switched to centre back in place of the suspended Zayette and Kilbane came in to the left back position. Brown also retained France in midfield and Doyle at right back as reward for decent displays at Newcastle.

The Gunners were clearly up for this game as they started with a physicality not normally seen from the North Londoners. Actually, with not a British player among the first eleven perhaps they should lose the right to be called Londoners. Arsenal played very directly, again this was unusual for Wenger's cultured crop. We coped pretty well against the better side and France's addition in midfield helped us break up much of the Arsenal rhythm and restrict them to few chances in open play. Disappointingly we conceded from a corner as Adebayor rose above Turner to steer the ball home and put the visitors ahead but we continued to work hard and went into the break just the one goal down. For all our hard work and industry it was obvious that we lacked creativity, especially with a 4-5-1 formation. It was especially important to make sure that any chances coming our way were taken. The introduction of Manucho meant that we switched to 4-4-2 and immediately looked more dangerous.

We are still running desperately short of luck at the moment as referee Alan Wiley refused to award a penalty for an assault on Manucho in the box. The player was left prostrate after

Djourou launched himself at the striker not the ball. It was an unbelievable decision but what can you do? Still we continued to press forward in search of the equaliser. When Mendy got the better of Clichey for once, he put in an inch perfect cross for Cousin to launch a powerful header into the back of the net. At 1-1 we looked the most likely to go on and win the game but Arsenal saved their best for last as their quality started to show.

Just as we were running out of steam, Nasri and Bentdnar both finished well to give the visitors a flattering victory. We had been condemned to our fifth consecutive defeat and our worst run of form since 1998. With all due respect to the teams we played over ten years ago, we are in a completely different league now in all senses of the word, it just wasn't comparable. What we needed to do was get back to winning ways as soon as possible against teams outside of the top six. These genuine six pointers would be our key to retaining Premier League status. Thankfully most teams below us were struggling at the same time. Paul McShane proved he's a Tiger at heart when he gave away a penalty to condemn Sunderland to a defeat against Villa. I bet Ricky Spragia is so pleased that he recalled the ginger wonder.

As the transfer window clock continued to wind down ex Liverpool defender Steve Finnan was almost signed but ultimately failed his medical causing City to pull out of the deal. This was probably a wise move given that Anthony Gardner has spent most of his time on the treatment table. Marlon King had a dressing room bust up with Phil Brown after being benched for the Arsenal game and looks like he has played his last for us. Wigan don't really want him back and are planning to swap him for Mido at Boro. This left us with two loan spots and a whole host of rumours and speculation about who we would sign next. While our chairman had to be prudent and select bargain buys, Manchester City's top man was quite literally trying to scatter cash everywhere. Despite offering a reported £107 million to Milan he couldn't get his hands on Kaka. At the same time Robinho was said to have left the team's warm weather training camp early without permission. It seems that money may not be able to buy everything after all. I've heard that the snappily named, Sheikh Mansour bin Zayed Al Nahyan is frustrated at not being able to offload any of his substantial wedge, so he has commissioned a select band of elite scientists from CERN (remember them?) to develop a time machine. Once the contraption is ready he intends to send Mark Hughes back to 1970 with explicit instructions to sign up Gordon Banks, Franz Beckenbauer and Pele. Did you know scientists have just found life on Mars? No really, they have.

Hull City 2 Millwall 0
FA Cup 4th round Saturday 24th January 2009

Remember when the FA went cap in hand to their Welsh counterparts in order to use their stadium? Cowboy builders were swinging the lead over the construction of the new Wembley and the FA had to borrow the Welsh national stadium. It was yet another embarrassing chapter in English football history but thankfully our own home of football ended up being ready for the Tigers first ever trip there.

I have been to the Millennium Stadium in Cardiff a few times including the 2004 FA Cup final and have to say it is a mightily impressive place. It is a little smaller than Wembley but when you think it was built at a fraction of the cost and comes complete with a sunroof, you can't help feeling that the FA should have used the same builders.

Manchester United took on the might of Millwall in 2004, on the face of it hardly a mouth watering prospect and probably the reason that there were a few spare tickets around. Little Dennis Wise took his merry band of men all the way to the final and although they were beaten soundly on the day, nobody can take the experience away from them. We were in among the Millwall fans and it was obvious that they had no intention of letting a 3-0 hammering spoil their day out as they sang from start to finish. There are four 'L's' in Millwall but their fans don't pronounce any of them. Hoards of tattooed, shaven headed, Bermondsey boys wearing Mr T style chains, fistfuls of sovereign rings, sleeveless T Shirts and cropped tracksuit bottoms, sang 'No one likes us, we are Miwaw, super Miwaw' over and over until their throats bled. It was quite an experience and ever since I have looked out for the results of one of the most unpopular teams in the Football League. After Wise did the dishonourable thing and left them high and dry they went through a sticky patch but under the guidance of ex

Watford and Swansea man Kenny Jackett, they seem to be having a bit of a renaissance. I was quite sure that they would be up for the cup when they faced us.

Something incredible happened the day before the game. We signed Jimmy Bullard. Mon Dieu, pardon my French but we really did sign Jimmy Bullard. Make no mistake this was a big deal. Bullard ranks amongst the best English midfielders in the country, don't take my word for it ask Fabio Capello.

City got the England squad member on a four and a half year deal for £5 million and a reported £40k a week but he could prove to be worth every single penny.

Just before kick off the Undertone's 'Jimmy Jimmy' rang out across the ground heralding the imminent appearance of our new star. He came out on to the pitch to rapturous applause and cheers from us and predictable boos and jeers from them. As he walked the ex Fulham man held a Tigers scarf aloft. To be honest I never thought I'd see the day when Hull City spent £5 million on a player.

Back to matters in hand, Millwall came at us directly from the kick off. Clearly Jackett's plan was to knock us out of our stride and disrupt our game and to an extent, it worked. The thing is though, we still remember having to play like that ourselves and although it didn't make for good football, we coped pretty well. Michael Turner popped up from an Andy Dawson free kick on the right to head us in front early in the game. Millwall huffed and puffed but didn't create too much. Their best chance's came from an indirect free kick inside the box, when Tony Warner was forced to handle a back pass. The resulting kick was skewed wide and when Neil Harris missed a point blank sitter just before the break, we got the feeling that it was going to be our day. The second half faired little better than the first but one moment of quality from Ian Ashbee secured the result for us. He coolly volleyed home from outside the box to make it two. That was it, as the Tigers saw off the

Lions quite comfortably in the end. The Millwall fans had no intention of going as meekly as their team had done though. It was as though they had borrowed the Sheikh's time machine and gone back to the bad old days of the 1980's. They ripped out seats and threw them at the city fans. Some of them returned fire in retaliation. According to eye witness reports one particularly hapless City fan was ejected for throwing his half eaten hot dog into the midst of the Lion's den. Apparently he was warned not to feed the animals but took no notice. The police moved in and seemed to adopt a policy of containment which was probably a wise move as they were outnumbered massively by three thousand, mostly hostile Londoners. After the final whistle Humberside's finest deployed mounted officers to ensure no one came on to the pitch. I bet the groundsman was chuffed at the thought of having to get hoof prints out of his prized turf. Apparently the hooligans demonstrated their affection for us northerners by wrecking large parts of the away end and running amok through the city centre as they headed back to the capital. No doubt there will be inquires and the like but this kind of thing needs to be stamped out before it gets hold again. My biggest fear is that the football authorities may do sweet FA.

In the home dressing room after the game, the City staff took stock after the on field battle. Andy Dawson fresh back from injury, sustained a nasty gash on his head and Zayette collected a broken nose for his trouble. I just hope it doesn't spoil his film star looks. Our prize for dispatching Millwall was a trip to beautiful downtown Bramall Lane and a realistic chance of making the quarter finals. Of course to achieve that we needed to steer a course past the old enemy and one thing was certain, a fifth round tie against the Blades would certainly not be for the faint hearted.

West Ham United 2 Hull City 0
Wednesday 28th January 2009

The City of Hull took another kicking during the week. A report came out claiming that Hull was badly placed to ride out the recession because of our low skills base. I was asked to appear on TV in support of the local college. Although I am terminally camera shy, I thought that this issue was worth talking about and I happily told reporter Tim Iredale, that things aren't as grim as they seem in Hull. In fact there is already a decent skill base here and with the colleges and others offering first class training opportunities, it could be possible for us to be ready for the upturn. Having done my best to stick up for Hull and secured my five minutes of fame, I proved beyond doubt that I have the perfect face for radio when my cameo appearance was featured on Look North and the Politics Show. Not bad going for someone who detests having his photograph taken.

Back to the big League with a trip to the East Ends finest, West Ham. I have to admit about being a bit nervous about this one.

The Hammers are a little bit like Man City, very capable of giving anyone a hammering on their day. There was also a rumour going round that the Millwall hooligans wanted to have another go at us and our trip to the East End represented an ideal opportunity for them. As it was, Green Street remained trouble free. It was a cold, dank, drizzly kind of day. The Bermondsey boys probably decided to stay at home with their feet up in front of the TV, while their mums got on with the tea. The Boleyn Ground or Upton Park as almost everyone prefers to call it is a great old place. It is home to a team who most football fans acknowledge, play the game the right way. Of course this dedication to football hasn't always gone well for the Hammers and silverware has been a little thin on the ground, especially in recent years. Upton Park was also the place that provided the spine of the England World Cup side in 1966. Geoff Hurst, Martin Peters and Bobby Moore, especially the England captain, loom large in West Ham folklore. Even though they have foreign owners West Ham still feels like a local team. The club has worked hard to emerge from the dark shadow of the time when their 'firm' had a fearsome reputation; it feels more like a family outfit now.

Despite coming in on the back of five straight League defeats the mood amongst the City supporters remained buoyant. There was still a belief that we could turn our slump round.

Our away support was great as always and we gave the Hammers fans a run for their money, even though they do belt out a decent rendition of 'I'm forever blowing bubbles,' now and then.

Unfortunately for us, on the pitch West Ham were as good as we were bad. They've hit a rich vein of form and continued to shine in this game we struggled to get near them. They hit the post early on and were awarded a dubious penalty when Carlton Cole ran out of space in the box and took the usual strikers option of going to ground. Fortunately for us, Matt Duke produced an excellent stop from Noble's spot kick. It was the first of many for Matt who went on to make a string of fine saves in the game of his life. Even Duke and the woodwork couldn't save us though, as the Hammers scored one in each half from Di Michele and Cole to run out comfortable winners. The only bright spot of the whole evening was the second half introduction of Jimmy Bullard. He certainly lifted the fans and the team but I was concerned at the amount of work he put in. His endeavour reminded me of Windass during his first spell at the club. Deano stood out back then and seemed to want to be at the heart of everything, I fully expected him to be serving the pies at halftime. I just hope that this current team isn't totally reliant on Bullard; otherwise we could be well and truly up the creek.

Why did we lose for the sixth League game in a row? Well simply put, they had better players; created more chances and scored more goals. More importantly, in the games when we have been totally outplayed so far, our opposition has functioned as a proper team. We needed to get back to those heady days of late summer when we also played as a team. There was still plenty of time left to get the required number of points for survival but with each passing defeat the odds were starting to mount against us.

We took our time and strolled back up to Upton Park tube station. All along Green Street pockets of West Ham fans shouted out, "Iron, Iron."

I was tempted to shout, "Any old," in reply but I thought better of it.

Once we got to the station there was a similar queuing arrangement to White Hart Lane, only the line appeared to go much further back. It seemed to me that most of the crowd had decided to get on the tube. We asked a local Bobby for directions to the next station but he couldn't help.

"I'm not from round here," he said.

He then went on to tell us that the line wasn't that long and it was moving quickly and it was our best bet anyway.

Well, it turned out to be a very long and extremely slow moving line. He lied like a cheap Chinese watch.

The journey home was thoroughly miserable; it always is when we lose.

Hull City 2 West Bromwich Albion 2
Saturday 31st January 2009

Daniel Cousin and Jimmy Bullard both picked up injuries from the West Ham game, so they weren't available for this one. As a result Marney retained his place and Phil Brown went for a previously untried partnership of Garcia and Fagan upfront. Unlike recent outings we certainly looked more like a proper team in this game. City dominated a clueless looking Baggies side and we took a well deserved lead on the back of some pretty comprehensive pressure. Just before halftime Ashbee volleyed a fine through ball for Mendy to latch onto. The Frenchman used his electric pace to round Scott Carson and coolly side foot home. If we continued the same way in the second half then we could end our poor run. That word 'if' is only two letters and one little syllable but it's actually a very big word when it comes to us. Albion came out fighting in the second half and levelled courtesy of a well taken goal from on loan Jay Simpson. We got wor noses in front again though, as Brownie would say. Mendy continued his first half battle with the Albion captain, Robinson. He managed to get the better of him and put in a difficult cross, when the easy ball was to Marney in acres of space. Fagan launched himself at the ball to head home and recapture the lead, what a goal. If we had just held our nerve and heads, that would have been it but there is that word again. Zayette went to ground in the box and the referee did what ref's always do in those situations and gave a penalty. Duke couldn't manage his heroics of earlier in the week and Brunt levelled the scores for a point. The Albion were delighted but it felt like two precious points dropped for us. After dominating so much of the game we deserved more than a point, that's for sure.

There was a lot of concern over Jimmy Bullard in the wake of the Albion game. He didn't feature and it turned out that he had collected a knee injury from his brief appearance at West Ham. The club had to wait for a report from the American specialist who operated on him eighteen months ago. This should determine the extent of the problem. Hopefully it would be good news; otherwise it could be a very expensive situation.

Wayne Brown followed Deano out of the door with his own loan move to Leicester and speculation mounted about two possible players coming the other way. The Italian international defender Panucci was one of the front runners among a list of many others and some of the usual suspects.

The transfer window shut and despite what we'd been promised there was no 'blow your socks off' signing.

It was disappointing but we had actually done a fair bit of business signing Bullard and Kilbane and bringing Manucho in on loan, while Stelios was another who had made for the exit door. We had also signed young French defender Steven Mouyokolo from Boulogne but he won't join until the summer. Arsenal appeared to be up to their old tricks as they signed Andre Arshavin, almost a full day after the transfer deadline. Quite how the Gunners managed to get round the rules I don't know but they do have history. In 1919 they were promoted to the top flight despite only finishing fifth in the second division in their previous campaign, same old Arsenal, eh?

Chelsea 0 Hull City 0
Saturday 7th February 2009

Last week it was all pie and mash and jellied eels, this week it would be cappuccino and espresso at every turn. The culture gap between East and West London couldn't be any wider. While West Ham can still lay claim to being a local club, Chelsea can definitely not. With a billionaire owner, an army of foreign players and a fan base almost as diverse as Manchester United, Chelsea are about as far away from a local team as you can get. We play them again straight after they have played Liverpool and again just after they have lost, what a coincidence. As I told you before I don't believe in those, so I was hoping we could break the pattern by getting something down at the Bridge. Scolari or 'Big Phil' as Welsh Phil calls him is having a tough time of it lately. He is finding it decidedly harder to manage a Premier League team than the Brazil national side. With those talented, fun loving Brazilians he managed to win the World Cup. Let's be honest though, my Granny could take Brazil to a World Cup. See, I told you she was versatile. The European players don't like his training methods and he seems to lack tactical ability. Scolari is in grave danger of coming up short on all fronts this season and that would surely signal the end of his English adventure.

Still the Chelsea boss must have looked at the fixture list and been relieved to see his side faced us at the Bridge next.

I was a bit worried about the journey down. We'd had a little bit of snow lately and the newsmen were talking it up to blizzard proportions. We seem to be lurching from terrorist threat, to financial meltdown, to ice age, on a weekly basis. It's obviously a government ploy to keep us all in line through fear. If we could just all calm down, then I'm sure everything would be alright. As it turned out the roads were clear and the trip to

London was smooth and uneventful, see what I mean? It's all a conspiracy.

It's not cheap to watch football these days, £47 a ticket was steeper than the away end at St James' Park. Even some Chelsea fans complained about the cost, not the prawn sandwich brigade I assume but the few real fans they have left. Let's be honest for that kind of money you could watch a proper show in the West End.

Stamford Bridge is not the place it used to be. The Chelsea village fronts the ground with a range of shops, apartments and a very posh restaurant run by Marco Pierre White. Old Marco is actually an Arsenal fan but presumably willing to put business before football allegiance. The infamous Shed End, scene of many a 'Chelsea Head Hunter' exploit, is now redeveloped along with the rest of Stamford Bridge to provide comfortable, modern viewing for the fans. Yet again there was great atmosphere inside the ground and again, most of it came from the City fans. I think we all knew we would be up against it but we were going to make the best of it and thoroughly enjoy the moment. Phil Brown kept faith with the same team that had done pretty well against West Brom but with Mendy out due to suspension Geovanni made a welcome return. A very nervous looking Scolari sent out his Chelsea team to face an improving City side. It's been a long time since our back to back wins in London but after going through a definite slump we now look hungry again. The Blues had plenty of possession but lacked a cutting edge in open play. A set piece saw John Terry sky a gilt edged chance over the bar and Duke made a good save to deny new signing Queresma in open play but that was as good as it got for them. We played with commitment, passion and above all balls. Zayette used his literally, to block a fierce free kick from Ballack, of all people. Honestly, it even made my eyes water, high up in the stand.

We went onto the concourse for a drink at halftime and the general feeling amongst everyone was that we could get something from this game. Fagan led the line extremely well all game and with some better finishing could have bagged a brace. Kilbane skimmed the post with a header and Marney dragged a shot a fraction wide of the same upright. Having scored a great goal against Millwall, Ian Ashbee had used up his luck quota and flashed a volley high and handsome in the closing minutes. John Terry led his disconsolate troop off at the end, knowing full well that they had been humbled by the Tigers but it could have been much worse.

Scolari had a face like a slapped arse on the sidelines and probably knew that his time was up. His name was added to the growing number of managers we have seen off lately but with a few million quid in his pocket, I'm sure the trip back to Portugal and away from the white hot pressure of the Premier League will be a pleasant one. Guus Hiddink would be next up in the hot seat at Stamford Bridge.

Although we didn't quite manage the win, it felt like we had. Of course everyone was saying that Chelsea are poor at the moment but while that is true, there was no denying that we made them look so much worse with our high tempo all action game plan. To me this was the best match since the Arsenal game and we could take this rediscovered confidence into the forthcoming games with every hope of getting good results.

We went for a drink in a pub not far down the Fulham Road after the match. The conversation amongst most of the locals was the embarrassing state of affairs in Comrade Abramovich's domain but I overheard two other fans chatting about something else. The two old boys sat across the table gazing down into their pints talking about disgraced American swimmer Michael Phelps. One of them had a theory about why he swept the board at the Olympics and it had nothing to do with the drugs he'd recently been caught taking.

"Eighteen inch feet," he said.

"What?" Asked his mate.

"You know, great big feet, eighteen inches." He said holding his hands apart to illustrate his point like a fisherman talking about the one that got away.

"That's why he is unbeatable, feet like paddles," he continued.

"Yeh but that Aussie, Thorpe, he beat him didn't he?"

"That was years ago, Phelps was a young kid," he protested.

"Nineteen," said the mate.

"He was younger than that, I'm sure."

"No, nineteen inch feet, you can't beat that. Thorpe had bigger feet, that's why he won," he conclude, triumphantly holding his hands out like the fisherman who had just landed the biggest catch of the day. We stayed the night in London at the same hotel we used for our trip to Wembley, our lucky hotel. The four of us went for a meal at a restaurant nearby in Borough market and of course we all had fish.

Sheffield United 1 Hull City 1
FA Cup 5th round Saturday 14th February 2009

Once a year we get away from the kids to spend one night on our own. We book in to the Witchery in Edinburgh. The hotel is on the Royal Mile near the castle and famous for its gothic suites and fairytale restaurant. We've been going for the last few years and with our visit this year, we have completed the set and managed to stay in all of the rooms.

The writer of The Da Vinci Code, Dan Brown stayed in the same rooms for a week when they were shooting some of the scenes for the movie with Tom Hanks nearby. Brown is part of a long list of celebrities who have stayed at the hotel but as far as I know, the only one who has been conceited enough to scrawl his name on the floorboards in permanent marker. That's the Yanks for you, if they're not busy insulting waiters or invading sovereign states, then they're defacing sixteenth century buildings, without a care in the world. We didn't let a little bit of American graffiti spoil our day though. An early train the next morning meant that we didn't get much time to sample the delights of Edinburgh on this trip. The Tigers were the top priority and we had to get to Sheffield for the kick off.

Alice had come back to Hull for the weekend to look after Joe, so that meant she'd be joining us for the game. Yet another sell out for City but not for the Blades, as empty seats were very much in evidence at a lacklustre Bramall Lane. Obviously the credit crunch was hitting everybody hard but the Sheffield fans were staying away in their droves mainly because of recent results and their dissatisfaction with manager, Kevin Blackwell. The fact is that football fans are very fickle and despite being in the fifth round of the cup and fifth in the Championship, it seems that a lot of fans want The Blades manager out. While Blackwell suffered the derision of the fans and moaned about injuries, suspensions and having to play

Greg Halford as a makeshift striker, Phil Brown rang the changes for City. He rested a few players and brought in Anthony Gardner for the first time since Blackburn. I was beginning to think that gardener was his profession and not his name, as the injury prone star has struggled to recover. The ex Spurs mans return to the centre of our defence meant a switch to midfield for Zayette in a move many fans were looking forward to. We started like a side that had just met on the bus and lacked any sort of coherence. Sheffield were brighter and looked the most likely to score and didn't surprise anyone when Halford rose at the back post to head them in front. City started to get their act together and play better football. Zayette got the equaliser from an Andy Dawson free kick and we went into the break level. We looked a lot stronger in the second half but the Blades had their moments as both sides went in search of the winner to avoid the dreaded replay. That's the way it worked out though and a return tie at the KC was both sides reward for an afternoon of hard graft but little invention.

Milo had also gone to the game with a few of his mates and despite our warnings about the way the South Yorkshire police tend to manage football crowds, he managed to get a black eye, as the City fans were herded to the station. I hate to say 'I told you so' but I did.

I remember last season when we were chasing automatic promotion and they spoiled our day by beating us two nil. The Sheffield fans were perfectly happy with that and didn't give us any trouble. The police had other ideas though; we were herded to the station by storm troopers sporting all manner of riot control gear and ably assisted by devil dogs and mounted cavalry. It was just a little over the top I think, especially when you consider there were a sizeable number of families with children in the crowd, hardly hooligans.

Two things were bothering me after being held in the cup for the second time. There was the obvious damage to my pocket that yet another game would bring. There was also the fact that another match in an already crowded fixture list was the last thing we needed, when Premier League survival was at stake. The draw for the last eight became the last fourteen as other draws and outstanding replays caused severe congestion. Our own draw was the busiest of all. If we get past Sheffield we would face an away tie with either Arsenal or Cardiff or Burnley. I didn't fancy any of these options. The FA Cup probably represented Arsenal's best chance of winning something this season, Burnley have already taken bigger scalps than ours and it's never easy going to deepest, darkest Wales.

Hull City 1 Tottenham Hotspur 2
Monday 23rd February 2009

We once bought a George Foreman grill. After using it a few times it was consigned to a kitchen cupboard along with a sandwich toaster, an ice cream maker, a bread maker, a candyfloss maker and a soda stream. All of these items, (none of which would have looked out of place on Bruce Forsyth's conveyor belt) seemed like a good idea when we bought them. Sadly they stand idle now, unwanted and gathering dust but even they have seen more action than Jimmy Bullard has in City colours. I'm thinking of getting a T Shirt with the number 37 on the back and across the front, the words, 'I saw Jimmy in black and amber.' Obviously it will be a limited edition print. His thirty seven minutes at West Ham will be his only appearance for the rest of this season and probably a fair chunk of the next as well. The innocuous challenge from Scott Parker, the same player who was involved in the original injury, (how about that for a coincidence?) led to the news that no one wanted to hear. Jimmy had damaged his anterior cruciate ligament again and had gone to Denver for the reconstruction of his troublesome knee. The surgeon is confident that the operation was a success and we will see Bullard return as good as new. I hope that he is right because the consequences of the talented midfielder not coming back are dire. The whole deal is worth something in the order of £14 million and there is no insurance on a pre existing injury. Losing a player of Bullard's calibre before he has had chance to impress in City colours is also quite devastating. It's no good saying what we have never had, we'll never miss. Try telling that to a lottery winner who has lost his ticket. No one is suggesting that Fulham deliberately sold us faulty goods but after facing fierce criticism for letting Bullard leave Fulham, Mohamed Al Fayed must have skipped hand in hand with Roy Hodgson all the way from Craven Cottage to Harrods for tea and cakes. I only hope that Paul Duffen has kept his receipt.

Craig Fagan also had a knee operation but he should be back a lot quicker than our Jimmy. Looking forward not back we have had some good news amongst all the bad. Gardner came through the Sheffield game unscathed and looked set to face his old club for the first time. Cousin returned from a minor knee operation and Ian Ashbee was also back to reclaim his place from Zayette, who proved that he is not ready to fill the captain's boots just yet.

We needed to be at our very best against a Tottenham side who are struggling to recover from a terrible start to the season. Spurs do possess some very good footballers and are more than capable of giving anyone a game. Defence would be the key. If we could shut out the likes of Keane, Bent and Pavlyuchenko, then we could get a result, if not then it was doubtful that we would have the firepower to come from behind.

We dominated the opening proceedings but went behind after a quarter of an hour by virtue of some sloppy marking. Lennon collected the ball on the edge of the area from a short corner and in yards of space coolly slotted home for the opener.

We have a habit of conceding early goals that put us on the back foot. Unfortunately, there was no sign of this trend ending any time soon. We continued to play well, restricting Tottenham and creating so much ourselves. We got our reward with a goal from Michael Turner and were right back in it. At halftime we were looking good to go on and win the game. Spurs came out like a different side in the second period and sadly, so did the Tigers. City gave away possession cheaply and struggled to get out of their own half. Gradually we clawed our way back in to the game and Tottenham's relentless pressure subsided. The match looked to be heading for a draw but again slack marking left Woodgate free and able to power home a header for the winning goal. It was cruel, we didn't deserve to lose but that's football for you. We played very well against a side that can boast £100 million worth of talent. We certainly didn't look like the poor relations but without any real cutting edge in the final third of the pitch we are struggling for goals at the moment. It looks like Phil Brown had pinned everything on Bullard being fit and becoming our creative force from midfield. With that option gone the squad have to dig deep and quickly. The final few minutes of the match were closed out as Harry Redknapp jumped and gesticulated around the technical area looking like a melting waxwork dummy. Phil Brown could only shake his head, like the rest of us, in extreme disappointment. The mood among the supporters as we left the KC was fractious to say the least. There was a spat between fans as we crossed the car park heading back to Anlaby Road. An irate Chelsea tractor driver accused another fan of damaging his wing mirror and tempers flared. Maybe the driver should be a little more patient rather than trying to mow down pedestrians in his rush to get away, or at least consider swapping to something more manageable, like a Ford Fiesta. It's nail biting time down at the KC Stadium, that's for sure.

Back at work Phil added to the misery again. Once again he had watched the game from the corporate seats and yet again he'd seen us lose. He did admit through gritted teeth that we deserved a draw but that's scant consolation seeing that we have registered only one victory in seventeen League games.

Hull City 2 Sheffield United 1
FA Cup 3rd round replay Thursday 26th February 2009

Trying to second guess Phil Brown this season has been difficult to say the least. On the face of it with a vitally important league fixture against Blackburn up next, this cup game should see him field a reserve side. That's exactly what his old pal Sam Allardyce did for Blackburn's replay against Coventry. They ended up going out of the cup but they will be able to field a fresh, full strength outfit against us.

I went to the Official Supporters Club fans forum, hoping to glean some insight into the inner workings of Phil Brown's footballing brain. Unfortunately all I really found out was that Phil drinks Guinness and Paul Duffen prefers Chardonnay. The rest of the evening was the usual 'back slapping' exercise, with no really searching questions. The high spot of the event was an off hand comment from Duffen about Rugby League fans. As a result followers of the oval ball game came out in their droves to condemn the chairman. I think some of the more vociferous fans wanted Paul Duffen to be burnt at the stake for heresy. Not only was Paul wrong about RL fans literacy levels but he also seriously misjudged their ability to take a joke.

Phil Brown did ring the changes from the Spurs match. Boaz started in goal, Zayette and Doyle went back into defence. Halmosi, France and Mendy shaped up in a new look midfield and Folan and Barmby spearheaded the attack for the first time this season. It was an awful lot of changes but says much about our strength in depth because you couldn't really call it the reserve team. We started very well and put the Blades under a lot of pressure. The unfortunate Norton powered a header Alan Shearer would have been proud of, against his own bar and down on to the line. It was well over the line, miles over, just like Geoff Hurst's goal in 66. Actually it was too close to call but the linesman must have had some Russian blood in him because he had no hesitation in awarding the goal. Sheffield got back on level terms against the run of play with a neat Billy Sharp finish. The striker also appeared to be tripped in the box but was booked for diving. While Sheffield could claim to be disadvantaged by the two key decisions it may be that we are turning the corner in terms of luck as well as football. Halmosi scored his first goal from some exquisite build up work from Barmby to finish off the Blades. To be fair, with the quality of the final ball from little Nicky, even my granny…. and all that but take nothing away from the Hungarian, this may be the lift he needs to get his season going. So we were in the quarter final for the first time since the year I went to Wembley with my dad. Moreover because Arsenal and Burnley are a tie behind everyone else, we will be in the draw for the semi final for the first time since 1930, the year City took Arsenal all the way to a replay. This is turning out to be one hell of a season.

Hull City 1 Blackburn Rovers 2
Sunday 1st March 2009

Paul is another of my mates from work who is moving on to pastures new. He decided to really push the boat out and have his leaving do at Ceruttis. We went out the night before the game and had a great time. The food there was exceptional as always and the company was pretty good too. I was surprised to see Phil Brown, Paul Duffen and friends. among our fellow diners in the restaurant. Their party seemed in very high spirits and certainly not worried about the game the following day.

Brown's team selection raised a few eyebrows and not for the first time this season. After seemingly grabbing the shirt in the Sheffield game with a man of the match performance, Nicky Barmby was benched. We started the game with Geovanni and Garcia upfront. The manager seems to becoming more of a tinker man day by day. Surely we needed some consistency in the starting line up and equally in our performances. Big Sam must have thought all his birthdays had come at once when he saw the team sheet. Having taken over from Ince, Allardyce had improved Blackburn's fortunes but they were only part way through the transition into his style of team and as such they were still beatable.

We started brightly and for half an hour looked the better side. Against the run of play we committed football suicide yet again though. Matt Duke failed to collect the ball allowing Santa Cruz to knock back for an easy Warnock tap in. That was bad enough but within a minute we were down by two as Blackburn took advantage of the referee's inability to find his arse with both hands, let alone find fault with Santa Cruz's mauling of Michael Turner. Keith Andrews of all players, the man who wasn't good enough for us in the Championship, took advantage and scored the goal that effectively ended the game.

Phil Brown waited until the hour mark to make changes, at last he brought on Barmby and Cousin but in taking off Geovanni he incurred the wrath of the crowd as the boos echoed around the stadium. While it was true that the Brazilian has been having a lean time, he always looks dangerous. He is one of the few players we possess who is capable of conjuring up something special when we need it most. The petulant way the player reacted to being hauled off was very telling. Our manager could be loosing the dressing room as well as everything else just now. Thinking back to the Manchester City game, it seems like the managers halftime dressing down on the pitch may be backfiring to some extent after all.

Blackburn continued to play a physical 'Sam Allardyce' type of game and when Pedersen brought Marney down yet again in midfield, the City player finally saw red and marched for lashing out. There was no way back now, for sure.

Pedersen got his comeuppance with a second yellow later and the levelling of numbers seemed to spur us on in the final few minutes. A well taken goal from Ashbee gave us hope but it was all too little, too late again as the game faded away.

The master most certainly got the better of his pupil on this occasion. I can't help thinking that big Sam was probably tucked up in bed early with a mug of cocoa and his Hull City file on the eve of the game. The press conference after the match was very telling. Phil Brown looked a worried man. The swagger and confidence seemed to have drained from him and he looked a shade or two lighter than he did before the match. Not only are the results not forthcoming but morale seems very low. The Manager will certainly need to earn his money over the coming weeks to turn this round. We haven't won in the League for a perilously long time and having wasted chances to put safe distance between us and the strugglers in the last two matches, we are now in deep trouble.

Everyone was starting to look at us and wonder what has happened to the team that took the Premier League by storm in the first half of the season. The fans would like to know as well.

Obviously there was only one thing for it as far as I was concerned; my beard would have to go. It had worked a treat in the first half of the season but it seems as though my facial hair had run its course as a good luck charm. The manager and the players had got rid of theirs ages ago, so for the good of the team I would have to lose mine as well. I know it sounds ridiculous but having lost the last two desperately important games I was willing to try anything.

This is turning out like the kind of roller coaster ride you wish you could get off. Everyone is feeling decidedly nervous and queasy as we are approaching the biggest drop of the lot.

Fulham 0 Hull City 1
Wednesday 4th March 2009

This was our last League trip to the capital but we may still have to visit Arsenal again in the cup unless Burnley can swing a major surprise and then who knows, Wembley beckons maybe? This also had all the makings of our most difficult game in London to date. Fulham have an impressive home record and are only second to Manchester United on that form.

By comparison we can't buy a win in the League at the moment. Dave had decided to come up from Portsmouth for this game, so we arranged to meet him at the Eight Bells near Putney Bridge station. There was a good mix of Fulham and City fans at the pub as we stood outside in the cool spring evening, discussing the beautiful game over a pint or two. What could be better?

We got talking to a Norwegian teacher, who was over here with some exchange students.

"We wanted to see a Premier League game, so we got tickets to watch Fulham play Hull City," he said.

"We are in the away end but if Hangeland scores, we may have to cheer."

"Don't worry," I said.

"That's not going to happen tonight."

"Are you a big Fulham fan then?" I asked.

"No, I am a Leeds United fan," the Norwegian boasted out loud.

"Sshh," I said.

"It would be best if you kept quiet about that."

We enjoyed a few more drinks in the build up to the kick off.

One city fan I was talking to told me that he was one of the few. For those in the know, that's the few fans who have been in away direct for the six years since it started. Paul Duffen has scrapped the scheme for next season but has promised that those fans will be looked after in recognition of their commitment to the club. That's all well and good but unless the club run a loyalty scheme they will run the risk of losing the fantastic away support we have now. I'm sure loyal fans will be able to get a ticket for a midweek game at Fulham but tickets for Saturday afternoon at Anfield will be much harder to come by. Die hard city supporters will inevitably lose out to star gazers who are more interested in watching the likes of Steven Gerrard than Ian Ashbee.

We made our way to the Putney end of Craven Cottage. The away stand is one of those pre fabricated things and the area behind the stand is shared between home and away supporters.

There was a friendly, family club atmosphere and although I couldn't see this kind of thing working at Stoke, it made a welcome change. We also shared the stand with Fulham fans and looking across to the tunnel, I noticed that some fans get to sit on the balcony of the actual Cottage in the corner of the ground. It seemed odd, a bit like the Royal box at the theatre. Given Al Fayed's well publicised views on that particular family though; I couldn't see Prince Philip sat there cheering Fulham on.

Phil Brown looked like he had picked an attacking line up for this game. Cousin and Fagan started upfront and Geovanni also featured. It seems as though manager and player have kissed and made up. The City fans gave their manager a rousing welcome as he walked in front of us with the backroom staff over to the dugout. He acknowledged our support with a raised fist. There was no doubting that we would be up for the fight in this game. Fulham's home record is no fluke. They have a good team, a good manager, they play good football and they are very hard to beat. Almost predictably, Fulham had the lion's share of possession and most of the chances. Geo came closest for us with a long range free kick in the first half. We restricted Fulham to long range efforts themselves and were pretty comfortable at the break.

The second half saw Fulham turn the screw. Matt Duke pulled off a string of fine saves to keep us in the hunt.

A draw looked the likeliest result as the game wore on. Brown introduced Garcia and Manucho for the tiring Cousin and Geovanni. Garcia went on a surging run before whipping in a cross for the unmarked Angolan to tap home the easiest of chances. The City faithful went wild. I'd have been happy with a point but in the end we nicked all three. Our record in London this season is phenomenal. We've won three, drawn one and lost only one. If I'd have predicted that at the start of the season, I'd have been measured up for one of those jackets with the wrap around sleeves. As it is, I'm thinking of writing to the Premier League to ask if we can play in London every week and bugger the expense. The reaction after the final whistle was amazing, fans jumping up and down, hugging each other. The players got in on the act as well. This is a united team and they want to remain a Premier League outfit and they want to do it for the fans. This result meant so much to everyone involved; it was like winning the Champions League.

Hull City 1 Newcastle United 1
Saturday 14th March 2009

With a week off, thanks to Arsenal and Burnley being a round behind everyone else in the FA cup, City had plenty of time to get ready for what would, according to Michael Owen, be our own cup final against Newcastle. Unfortunately for me, a week with no football meant that I started to take more notice of the financial gloom and doom. The Bank of England in conjunction with the government has come up with a cunning plan to kick start the economy though.

In addition to cutting the base rate to 0.5% they will create an extra £75 billion in order for people to start buying things again. I'm no financial expert but I know a bit about history and the last time people started to print extra money in Europe, it resulted in your average German having to use a wheelbarrow full of cash just to buy a loaf of bread. The new plan is known as 'quantitative easing,' or in football terms 'hit and hope.'

It's not all bad news at the moment though. The Queen came to Hull to bestow some royal goodwill on our much maligned City. She had lunch at the Guildhall and got to meet Phil Brown among the invited guests. Hopefully she gave him a few pointers for the vital weeks ahead and discussed the relative merits of four, four, two over a cucumber sandwich and a cup of Earl Grey.

Despite our win at Fulham, most pundits still think we'll go down. In fact from day one, they have been desperate for us and the other two promoted teams to fail. I watched Football Focus and saw Martin Keown put on the spot about the possible relegation fodder. The former Arsenal centre back, who would surely command a place in any 'ugly eleven,' thought for a second. Thinking, along with modelling, is clearly not a task that big Martin is well equipped for because he took the easy way out and blurted us, Stoke and West Brom as the teams who will go down. While West Brom unfortunately do look doomed the same can't be said yet for us or Stoke for that matter. There are other teams who look in a great deal more trouble than us and the Potters but we're not big names are we Martin?

Arsenal eased past Burnley to make the quarter final date with us in the cup and we both went into the draw for the semi finals. It seemed very strange to see ourselves up there but it's yet more evidence of an astonishing season. If we do manage to overcome the Gunners it will be another date at Wembley to take on Chelsea. I disagree vehemently with playing the semis at our national stadium, It takes the shine off the final but I suppose the FA have to try to pay for their folly somehow. If we manage to conjure up a victory over the Blues, we would then most likely have to play Manchester United in the final, again at Wembley. A relatively easy route to cup glory, I'm sure you'll agree.

With only Bullard and Boateng on the injury list, Phil Brown had the luxury of an almost complete squad to choose from.

He took the sensible option of trying to get some stability into the side by picking the same starting eleven who had done so well at Fulham. His plan certainly worked well in the first half. We looked brighter and the more likely to score. Geovanni worked well to lay the ball off to Craig Fagan who returned the ball with a superb left footed cross to the far post. Geo rose majestically to steer the ball past Harper in the Newcastle goal, for our first home lead in a very long time.

City looked comfortable against a pretty poor Magpie attack. Owen, fresh back from injury, looked tired and Martins who claimed he didn't know where Hull was, clearly didn't know where the goal was either. It was left to a defender to level the scores. The Tigers own solid defence lapsed momentarily. By allowing Nicky Butt far too much room to whip in a curling cross which Steven Taylor was able to finish with a very neat volley. The lad might not be a very good defender, according to Ronaldo but he showed Newcastle's front two the way it should be done. Both teams huffed and puffed in the second half with our best chance coming when Bernard Mendy got into a great position to cross the ball to either the advancing Manucho or the even better place Fagan. Unfortunately the Frenchman appeared to be caught in two minds and with both of them apparently feeble, he ended up putting the ball far too close to Harper for an easy take.

"Allez Bernard, for God's sake allez."

The game faded as both sides ended up settling for the draw. The solitary point certainly suited us better as we moved a couple of places up the table and left Newcastle still floundering. Michael Owen had heaped pressure on himself and his team by describing this as a 'must win game.' So that means that Newcastle are doomed then, doesn't it?

Arsenal 2 Hull City 1
FA Cup Quarter Final Tuesday 17th March 2009

Joe wrote five short stories for Comic Relief, each one was about someone in his family, thinly disguised as other characters. The stories ranged from superhero cousins to Milo the monkey, who Joe described as 'one crazy monkey gone bananas.'

I ran off a few copies, we sent them to friends and family and asked them to make a donation to Comic Relief if they wanted to. Joe's stories managed to bring in £85 for the charity. I'm an extremely proud dad, not only because of the money he raised but also because his writing is much better than mine.

We went to The Emirates with renewed confidence from the last couple of League matches. I was optimistic that we could get a result in this game; my pal Phil on the other hand predicted a 2-1 defeat, just to annoy me of course.

On the tube to Arsenal I was stood next to a couple of Gooners. We were joined at Russell Square by two Chinese supporters wearing Arsenal scarves.

"Are you going to the match," said one Chinese fan.

"Yes we are," replied the Gooner.

"Are you Hull City fans?" Asked the other Chinese fan.

"Yeh, yeh, we are Hull," said the Gooner.

"You are doing well, what have you got, twenty eight points?"

"Yeh, twenty eight."

I couldn't stand it any longer.

"We've got thirty three," I said.

"Ah, you a Hull fan as well?" Asked the Chinese fan.

"Yeh, I am but these two aren't, they don't even know where Hull is."

"I don't care where Hull is," said one of the freshly outed Gooners.

"Have you come down for the game?" He continued.

"Yeh we follow our team everywhere," I said.

"That's good, I respect that," said the Gooner.

I think that was the last respect we got all evening.

Phil Brown made one or two changes but still started with a very strong side and from the off they took the game to Arsenal. The evergreen Nicky Barmby rolled back the years with a vintage performance. Little Nicky got the opener with an excellent finish over the goalkeeper from the left flank. He also popped up on the right to slot home an Andy Dawson cross but was adjudged fractionally offside. Geovanni looked back to something like his best, producing one of his trade mark free kicks which needed a wonder save from Fabianski to stop it bursting the onion bag.

We reached the break one up and deservedly so. Spirits were high amongst the City faithful. We all hoped that we could repeat our first half performance but we were realistic enough to know that Arsenal would come at us in the second half and that we would have to weather a storm to emerge victorious.

Hughes replaced the injured Ashbee at halftime and we inevitably lost a bit of bite in midfield but City continued to cope pretty well with Arsenal's pretty play. The Gunner's decided to do what they had done at the KC stadium and revert to 'route one.' The pressure paid off as we entered the last sixteen minutes of the game as Van Persie's effort finally beat Myhill. Arsenal won the game with a Gallas goal in the final few minutes. The fact that the Frenchman was clearly stood a good yard offside when the long ball was delivered escaped the attention of the linesman and everyone's favourite referee, Mike Riley.

To go out to Arsenal, at their place, in the quarter final of the FA Cup was no disgrace but to do it by virtue of such a shocking decision, was a very bitter pill to have to swallow. Same old Arsenal. As we left a senior steward harangued a young city supporter for climbing over Arsenal's plush seating.

"Leave him alone," I said.

"You've won the game, show some humility."

The steward just smiled.

After the final whistle the Arsenal captain Fabrigas, came on to the pitch. He strode around like a feral youth seemingly looking for confrontation. Brian Horton alleges that the young Spaniard found trouble when he spat at the City number two in the tunnel. Amidst accusations and denials Phil Brown went public about the incident and also the poor officiating. It seems likely that there will be trouble ahead for the Tigers boss as the fallout settles. As far as the team goes though, this performance should give us good cause for optimism. We played without fear. We had our moments and but for a shocking decision, we could have nicked a replay. Back at work Welsh Phil was quick to remind me that his prediction was correct, Arsenal had won 2-1 after all. I just smiled.

Wigan Athletic 1 Hull City 0
Sunday 22nd March 2009

The furore following our cup exit at the Emirates showed no signs of easing. There's no doubt that the alleged actions of Fabrigas are being questioned but so to is the way that Phil Brown reacted. He is widely accused in the media of falling for his own hype and dragging the club with him. We are rapidly moving from everyone's favourite team to laughing stocks. Perhaps Phil should take a leaf out of Tony Mowbray's book. The West Brom boss manages to keep a dignified silence for the most part, despite being in a far more perilous position than us. It all comes down to respect and the FA's much heralded respect campaign is now in complete tatters.

Like us Wigan share their ground with a Super League club. Their pitch seems to hold up a lot better than ours though and that may have something to do with the fact that the JJB Stadium has four proper stands and open corners which allow air and sunlight to get in. Their team is also doing much better than ours. One more win would put them on 41 points and ensured of safety but the way they are playing then surely Europe isn't out of the question. As Bruce Forsythe used to say, "Points make prizes."

Having being embroiled in a survival battle for the last few years, I'm sure that their current position gives everyone at the club a warm feeling. It's clearly something we should aspire to.

City went into the game without our influential captain who shares the injury room with Gardner and Cousin. A reshuffle of the pack was in order but by picking Kilbane for centre midfield and giving him the captain's armband, not to mention leaving Nick Barmby on the bench, surely our manager was bluffing.

We got absolutely battered in the first half. Wigan must have had a dozen clear cut chances and only their failure to convert any of them kept us in the game. Honestly, if it had been a boxing match, the referee would have stopped it. The difference between the teams was twinned with the gulf between supporters. In comparison to poor, lacklustre Latics support, City's away following was, not for the first time this season, outstanding. We certainly did our very best to lift the players. Alice caught the train from Manchester to join us and as usual she got into the spirit of things by giving her vocal chords plenty of hammer. I gave Dave a call at halftime.

"Does it look bad on Sky?" I asked.

"It's not as good as that," said Dave.

Alice and Joanna went on to the concourse for a drink. I was driving so I couldn't even drown my sorrows with them.

The team did perform better in the second half, let's be honest; they could hardly have played worse. Our strikers at least gave Kirkland something to do other than his stretching exercises. It must have looked to Steve Bruce as though their chances had come and gone and it wasn't going to be their day. An unlikely draw looked on the cards for us until Marney and Duke conspired to allow Ben Watson to take the win. Brucie must have been both relieved and delighted.

"Good game, good game," I imagined the pudding faced Brucie chirping to himself.

Referee Andre Mariner was subbed by the fourth official, Mike Dean with only a couple of minutes to go. What kind of injury would mean he couldn't finish the game off so late on? Maybe he was just fed up. If he was as disappointed with the quality of the football as I was, then he has my complete sympathy and understanding but at least he was getting paid to watch.

I felt cheated after the match not because we lost and not even because it was a poor advert for Premier League football. No, I felt cheated because of the team selection. I don't know if the pressure is getting to the manager but he shouldn't be gambling now. We need a steady hand and cool nerves to stay at the top table. Anthony Gardner was diagnosed with having four cracked vertebrae from his brief spell as striker late in the Arsenal game. The treatment for this type of very unusual injury is complete rest so even gardening is out of the question for the unlucky defender. He certainly won't be pulling up any trees on the pitch until the start of next season at the earliest.

The international break has probably come at the best possible moment for us. The time off should allow City to re-group and get some of the walking wounded back for the final push. There are eight games to go and at a conservative estimate four are winnable but only if we start with our best team and set out to win. This is no time for faint hearts.

In the absence of a match at the weekend I decided to go to see 'The Damned United.' It's a film based on David Peace's book of the same name. The story centres on Brian Clough's turbulent forty four days at the helm of Leeds United. Where Peace's book paints a very dark picture of Clough, the film has a more balanced approach. Neither version is completely factual though. You can't let the truth get in the way of a good story. Hollywood has been doing this for years but the genre is now known as 'Faction.' Why does everything need to have a label? Michael Sheen plays Clough to near perfection.

His observational skills are so good that I actually believed I was watching Brian Clough as he battled against one of the earliest examples of 'player power.'

Sheen's football skills aren't too shabby either. My favourite part of the film is when Clough takes his first training session at Elland Road.

"Pay attention Irishman, you might learn something," he shouts addressing Johnny Giles.

"251 goals in 274 starts." He picks up the ball and starts to juggle it with both feet, up to his head and down for a perfect turn and right footed volley into the back of the net.

"I'd like to see Don Revie do that," he said as the stunned and silent assembly of Leeds United greats looked on.

I wanted to jump up and shout, "Yes….Get in there." I really did. Brian Clough was one of my great heroes. Along with others like John Lennon, George Best and Muhammad Ali, Clough represents the time I grew up in. Like them he had an arrogance underpinned with supreme ability. He was without doubt the greatest football manager England never had. If only the old duffers at FA headquarters had possessed the nerve to appoint him, we probably wouldn't have been through so many years of pain with our national team.

I met John McGovern a couple of years ago at work; he'd been booked to do some motivational speaking. Obviously he was able to draw on the lowest point of his career, his difficult time at Leeds especially when Clough had gone. He went on to talk eloquently also about the zenith of his career, 'The Great Escape' season working alongside Warren Joyce at City.

He mentioned something about lifting consecutive European Cups under Brian Clough at Nottingham Forest as well I think.

Chris Waddle was the latest to throw his oversized hat into the football ring. He described us as being in freefall and sure to replace his beloved Newcastle as the third team to go down along with Boro and West Brom. Waddle has proved that he is as adept at punditry as he is at taking penalties, remember Italia 90? Have they found that ball yet? Chris should know that 'it's not over until the fat lady sings.' Maybe it's the distant echoes from singing with Glen Hoddle on Top of the Pops all those years ago that are confusing him.

As with everyone else in the football world, Waddle must have been surprised with appointment of Alan Shearer as Newcastle manager for the rest of the season. It turned out to be true and not a grand April fools joke. With Joe Kinnear on his sick bed and Chris Hughton out of ideas, owner Mike Ashley had to do something. Shearer will get paid handsomely for his efforts and in all honesty he can't fail. If they go down it won't be his fault and he'll pocket a huge pile of cash. If they stay up, he will be hailed as a messiah on Tyneside and pocket an even bigger pile of cash. I'm sure he will inspire the fans but let's be honest; they're easily pleased up there. If Charlie Chaplin was a Geordie they would have welcomed him as a Manager at some point. Motivating their shambles of a team will be a different matter for the man who appears to have all the Charisma of a wet afternoon in Scunthorpe. Let's be honest, Shearer is not the messiah, he's just a very ordinary man.

Dean Windass turned forty on April 1st and he's back at the club, playing and scoring for the reserves and hopefully getting involved in some coaching capacity for the first team. He could do a lot worse than teach the strikers how to keep the ball down when shooting. Phil Brown welcomed Windass back with open arms but put restrictions on his media work. A case of 'pot calling kettle black' there maybe.

It's been a long two weeks since our last game. Having a lot of time on my hands, I've been forced to turn my attention to other things. Barack Obama was in the capital with the other G20 leaders trying to find a way out of this financial mess.

There is an awful weight of expectation on him; it's like bringing on Windass against Chelsea when you're 3-0 down. He's good but I'm not sure he's that good. All of our government departments appear to be failing spectacularly at the moment. The economy, health service and education systems are in turmoil and sport is no different. Despite surely having enough on his plate with the 2012 Olympics and a 2018 World Cup bid, Andy Burnham has launched a government initiative. Local councils are being encouraged to admit over 65's and under 16's free to their swimming pools. I hope the minister is also willing to fund the massive extra quantity of chlorine that will surely be needed.

Part of what I do in my job involves working with Angolan apprentices. They are a great bunch of lads, keen as mustard and football barmy. I contacted Danny Pratt at City to see if we could arrange a visit with Manucho. I thought it would be good for the player and the lads to be able to have a chat in their mother tongue for a bit. We arranged to meet up at the College at the Queens Gardens site. The event went extremely well and I'm sure everyone concerned will get good publicity from it. More importantly I think that Manucho should get a big boost from knowing that so many of his fellow countrymen are routing for him.

The Portsmouth game ended up being a bit of a non entity really. Defences were fully on top and opportunities were at a premium at both ends. City's best chance came as Craig Fagan steered a decent header towards goal and David James cleared with a fine reaction save. At the other end Duke had even less to do than the England number one but was caught flat footed as Pompey almost nicked it at the death with Hreidarsson's header scraping the foot of the post. The only other real excitement came courtesy of a Glenn Johnson dismissal. Johnson was clearly pumped up for this game as he ran amuck with some very reckless challenges in the first half. Referee Foy did yellow card him for a swipe at Zayette but he let pretty much everything else go unpunished. To be fair Johnson settled down a bit in the second half but ended up being sent off in bizarre circumstances. Marney stuck his foot out in front of the advancing Johnson and went over. The referee thought he had seen enough and promptly issued a second yellow for essentially nothing. As is so often the case, we didn't take advantage of the extra man and the stalemate remained unbroken. It certainly wasn't a good advert for the Premier League but when you are at this stage of the season everyone is bound to be nervous. It was a point in the end and as Shearer failed to have the immediate impact expected up on Tyneside, we moved a point further away from the bottom three.

Middlesbrough 3 Hull City 1
Saturday 11th April 2009

Four thousand City fans travelled north for just about the shortest trip of the season to the Riverside, amidst the cooling towers and distillation columns of the once great Imperial Chemical Industries. As must win games go this was the most must win game so far, particularly for Boro. If they fell to us, they would surely be down. In a bid to get the Middlesbrough fans squarely behind the team, their marketing department stayed up all night to come up with a 'Hull of a deal.'

The stadium was packed with two for one ticket offers, school kids on freebies and from what I could tell from looking at the gurning locals, the entire population of Royston Vasey.

Gareth Southgate certainly set up his team to go for the win. He chose King and Alves up front and played Tuncay in a central midfield role. Conversely Phil Brown picked a 4-5-1 formation. You could argue that in a midfield which included Mendy, Fagan, Barmby and Geovanni, City had plenty of attacking options but it was clear that Phil was going for a must not lose policy. Ex City bad boy Marlon King had an excellent game and silenced those who had tried to taunt him with chants about his private life. Gradually the chanting faded as King started to get the better of Turner. It came as no surprise that the striker was instrumental in the first goal. His shot could only be parried by Duke straight into the path of the equally impressive Tuncay for the opener. We got back on level terms quickly as Barmby crossed from the right for Manucho to deliver a perfect header into the back of the Boro net. Our relief was short lived though. Ian Ashbee ran the ball along the touchline before clearing down field. Unfortunately the linesman reckoned the ball went out. It didn't look as though it had but the way we defended from the resulting corner was no excuse. Bates turned the ball in at ground level completely unmarked for his first ever Boro goal. He'll never score an easier one.

"When was the last time we scored three goals in one match," I said to Joanna as I wondered if we could win the game.

"Man United."

"God, that seems like a long time ago," I said reappraising the match and realising that a draw was probably the best we could hope for.

Even with so much at stake we made little progress in the second half. At one point Manucho found himself wide left and delivered an inch perfect cross to no one. Obviously the fact that he was supposed to be the sole striker up top had escaped him. Brown switched things by bringing on Folan and Marney and going 4-4-2 and as a result we did look a bit better but with still with no reward. Our last throw of the dice was to bring on former Boro favourite Boateng. He got a good reception from the home fans and looked the most progressive of our midfield players. Unfortunately for George he was caught in two minds at the back and King took advantage to receive the ball and seal the victory with a well deserved finish.

He held his hand up to his ears after scoring but heard nothing; there's never been a better way to silence your critics than putting the ball in the back of the net.

We were to be kept back after the game as the police waited for the unusually large home crowd to clear. We were in no mood to stay and along with others found one of the turnstiles and gates unlocked. We made good our escape and started on the journey back still seething at what we had witnessed.

Phil Brown is a very analytical manager. He believes passionately in ProZone and all the statistics that their system provides. I also believe in learning from what has happened but I go a bit further back than the last game. What we are doing in the second half of the season is almost exactly what Sheffield United did a couple of seasons ago. Just like Warnock, Phil

Brown seems nervous. Just like the Blades, the Tigers are mostly playing a system to try not to lose.

Just like United, City are finding it's not working and just like them we could come up short.

To add insult to injury Marlon King sent his man of the match bottle of champagne to Phil Brown afterwards. I hope Phil hasn't cracked it open. He will be able to return it with interest if Boro' go down and we some how manage to stay up.

Sunderland 1 Hull City 0
Saturday 18th April 2009

A quick return to the north east took us to a place nestled between smog bound Middlesbrough to the south and the metropolis of Newcastle to the north. A visit to Sunderland is almost like a step back in time. Street urchins run wild, making mischief and darting in-between sour faced adults who shuffle along dark, Dickensian streets. Sunderland is also the only place I have seen white dog crap since I was a kid. What further proof do you need that the Mackems are firmly routed in the past as they cling forlornly to former footballing glory?

We'd been to the Stadium of Light a couple of seasons ago when Roy Keane's revolution was in its infancy. Finn was the City mascot. He got to run out with his heroes in front of the biggest crowd we had seen in a long while. Phil Brown was also in the early days of his career as City boss and our fortunes couldn't have been more different. We battled relegation and the Black Cats flirted with promotion.

Finn got to meet Niall Quinn who turned out to be a great bloke and Roy Keane who was just plain sullen.

"What do you think the score will be?" Roy said to Finn.

"If you say you're going to win, I'll not be happy."

"2-2," said Finn.

"I'm still not happy," said the stoical Irishman.

Sunderland ran out easy winners 2-0 and the rest is history.

I think I saw Keane smile after the match but looking back I think it could well have been wind.

The situation now is that we both find ourselves in the unenviable position of scrapping for Premier League survival in yet another must win game. Despite having lashed out many more millions than us in their quest for Premier League success, Sunderland look just as capable of going down as we do. Where we have struggled to get the quality needed, they seem to lack team spirit. Keane walked away apparently frustrated at the way the game has gone. He served under Brian Clough and Alex Ferguson, so getting the run around from Prima Donna players with far less ability or motivation than himself must be more than he can stomach. No one typifies the new order more than Djibril Cisse. He drives an American muscle car; it's a Dodge Phallus I think. At any rate it looks like a pimp's car and he dresses to suit as well.

He emerged from the burnt orange beast resplendent in a long black coat with a huge fur collar. Clutching a diamond encrusted iphone, he was instantly mobbed by the urchins, keen either to grab his autograph or pick his pockets. In all honesty he couldn't have looked much more like a pimp if he'd worn a leopard skin fedora and carried a pearl handled cane. I can't help feeling a bit sorry for Roy Keane.

Not for the first time Phil Brown went public with his thoughts. He inadvertently gave Sunderland a lift by criticising their underperforming stars. His opposite number Ricky Spragia, a man who has a face that quite bizarrely looks too big for his head, pinned the offending newspaper article on the home dressing room wall and sat back. It was noticeable that Anton Ferdinand exchanged a word or two with Phil Brown after the game. For the record I actually think he, in particular is overpriced. I mean he's ok but he's no Rio, is he?

In addition to criticising the Black Cats, Phil Brown also gave his own charges some stick, only this time he rightly kept his comments in house. It seemed to work. He brought Myhill back in and Kilbane into midfield to face another of his old clubs. We certainly looked the better side but still without having that cutting edge in front of the sticks. Against the run of play Cisse nodded in the flick on from Kenwin Jones take the lead in almost the last action of the first half. He was clearly offside but the linesman missed it. We continued to toil away in the second half but all the effort and industry came to nothing as Manucho and Folan and just about every other city player looked incapable of producing an accurate finish. George Boateng came the closest with a wicked drive that would surely have burst the onion bag, had it gone in. Jones had the ball in the net again for them but this time the other linesman was 'Johnny on the spot' and got the offside decision right. Mendy was lucky not to be sent off as his Gallic temper boiled over and he went head to head with Kieran Richardson. The final few nerve jangling minutes were played out with Sunderland rallying one last time and hitting the post from a Murphy effort. You'd have thought that they'd won the Premier League title, the way the Mackems reacted when Mike Dean blew his whistle. Sunderland are far from safe themselves but their fans wasted no time in rubbing salt into our festering wounds.

"I feel sorry for these poor lads having to go all that way home after that," said one fan for my benefit.

"It could be worse, I could live here," I replied.

They just laughed and went on their way.

Another older Mackem offered his support.

"Never mind canny lad, you could still stay up."

"So could you," I said reminding him that they are only a point above us and haven't actually won the Champions League yet.

"What's you're run in like?" He asked, ignoring my comments.

"Tough," I said,

"Liverpool, Villa and Man U all to come."

"Ah that's going to be hard, it's a good job you got that good start or you might have ended up like Derby," he said.

I'd had enough patronising for one day so I peeled off and left the self styled King of Europe to mutter on to himself.

The sad thing is that he could be right. Since December it's all gone wrong. It may be too much to hope that Boro, Newcastle and West Brom will continue to be worse than us. At least they were this week as most of the other results went our way.

Hull City 1 Liverpool 3
Saturday 25th April 2009

April 15th 1989 marked the darkest day in the history of Liverpool. The disaster at Hillsborough was commemorated recently. In the twenty passing years a lot has changed and so much more has happened but no one even remotely interested in our national game will ever forget that truly terrible day.

On the surface anything other than a sound thrashing seemed unlikely against a side that have scored twelve goals in their last three games. Mind you they had let a few in as well and we always seem to raise our game against the better teams, so fingers crossed. Kevin Kilbane replaced an injured Andy Dawson and Caleb Folan started up front in place of Manucho.

City started well and played a high tempo, pressing game. There was no doubt that we were taking the game to the big boys. Both sides had chances with the Reds coming closest when Torres forced a wonderful one handed save from Myhill.

We seemed to be functioning like a proper team again and everyone stepped up to the plate as Brownie would say. We more than matched the title chasers. Unfortunately for us, Liverpool were aided by referee Martin Atkinson. The West Yorkshire man allowed himself to be fooled by Mascherano's extravagant dive in front of Boateng. Alonso's free kick struck the wall and in the dying minutes of the first half, the Spaniard volleyed the rebound sweetly past the unsighted Myhill. For the second game running we had gone behind at the worst possible time as the result of poor officiating. The linesman on our side was almost as bad as Atkinson. He waved his flag like a demented semaphore signaller, at every available opportunity in favour of the Reds. Every time a Liverpool player brought his hand up to his head the man in black frantically waved a distress signal. I was frightened to blow my nose in case he penalised City.

Boateng went to have a word with the referee after he blew up for halftime, presumably to discuss the degree of difficulty on the Argentinean's dive. I've heard George speak, he is very articulate so I can't imagine that he went to abuse Atkinson but he was shown a yellow card for his trouble anyway. It's appalling that so many of our so called, 'top officials' are actually so very poor and also so very convinced that crowds turn up just to see them every week. I long for the days when referees were unknown quantity surveyors from Basingstoke.

We came out fighting in the second half and certainly looked as if we could get something from the game despite the crippling set back. We stuck to our task but when Folan chased down a ball into the box and was obstructed by Škrtel, he foolishly lashed out at the defender. Atkinson couldn't get his card out quick enough to send the striker off. It was a terrible shame not only for the team but for the player himself. Folan had been having one of his best games in a City shirt but this rush of blood cost him and the side very dear and was inexcusable. Everyone had been calling for Folan to show more aggression in games but more in a controlled way, not like some spoilt child.

We were really up against it now but we reshaped and stuck to our guns. Liverpool scored the inevitable second after breaking quickly. Kuyt finished well but not before the corner was taken outside of the line and then Lucas controlled the ball with his hand. The referee did an 'Arsen Wenger,' claiming he didn't see it and the goal stood. There really didn't look any way back for our ten brave battlers now. Brown subbed Barmby and Fagan for Cousin and Mendy and the injection of fresh legs certainly give us a boost. Mendy's Gerrardesque sixty yard cross field pass found Cousin who skipped past Skrtel and played an inch perfect cross for Geovanni to finish with ease. As unlikely as it seemed, we were back in the hunt. The nervy

Benítez sensed an upset so he threw on another defender in a clear case of 'we hold what we have.'

Liverpool hit us on the break as we went in search of an equaliser with Kuyt bagging his brace and ensuring an extremely flattering win for the Scousers.

Games to do were getting few and still there was no sign of those precious last few points that would ensure our Premier League survival. We certainly weren't getting much luck either. A quick look at former referee Jeff Winter's League of Injustice shows that we should be about five points better off and sitting comfortably in twelfth place, if only the laws of the game had been correctly and consistently applied. It seems that some teams get the lion's share of everything. When you are up against the best you don't need to be playing the refs as well.

On the up side there were plenty of positives to take out of the game. Geovanni was up for the fight and had one of his best games for quite a while. Marney too seemed to have recaptured some of his earlier form. Our defence looked pretty assured and solid and typified the spirit that ran through our side. If we play like this in our remaining games we should be fine.

There's that bloody word again, if.

Ex Liverpool hero, Kenny Dalglish gave us all the benefit of his wisdom after the game. The humourless Scotsman predicted that his former club Newcastle would pip us to survival, on goal difference. Well Kenny and his cronies won't have long to find out now, will they?

Aston Villa 1 Hull City 0
Monday 4th May 2009

Dean Windass was finally shown the door at the KC stadium. His departure was shrouded in secrecy and silence. The club have agreed to pay up his contract up and told him to stay away. It's no good speculating about what might have happened it's all just a very sad and unfortunate end to our local hero's career.

Villa Park is another of those old 'Stately Home' type of grounds. Rich in History and crumbling splendour, the place is steeped in footballing history. Until recently it was the prime choice for FA Cup semi finals. Of course the FA's folly at Wembley has put paid to that sort of thing for the foreseeable future. Inside it has been updated and improved and under Martin O'Neill the club are fashioning a footballing side fit to grace their illustrious surroundings.

With the big three in the North East all getting well beaten at the weekend and West Brom's one win mini revival over, City had an opportunity to put further daylight between themselves and the others. After such a good team effort against Liverpool surely Phil Brown would play the same side as far as possible.

Not a bit of it, he actually made several changes. Second guessing our manager has become a difficult pastime these days. A couple of changes were forced on him by injury or suspension but why bring Ashbee straight back in and why drop Barmby and why play the dreaded 4-5-1 formation?

I think we all wanted to know but I also think there was more chance of me getting the answers than Radio Humberside's sporting correspondent. Burnsy upset the increasingly touchy manager by asking similar questions a week earlier.

We started reasonably well. The idea was obviously to contain and defend and then try to sneak a goal a little bit like the plan at the earlier fixture at the KC.

The quick return for the captain backfired when he went off after a full blooded challenge with James Milner. It looked like knee damage, if it is then that's his season gone and the rest.

Coming on, Marney looked incapable of repeating his performance of a week earlier. For their part Villa looked every inch the top five side that they are. Passing and movement was neat, fast and crisp and the finishing wasn't too shabby either. It would be fair to say that over the course of the game, Myhill kept us in the hunt with a vintage performance at his old ground. We had a couple of half chances but failed to put Freidal under any real pressure. Geovanni lined up to take a free kick about 35 yards from goal.

"Shoot," I shouted insincerely.

The diminutive Brazilian shaped up with an extravagant run in, reminiscent of Roberto Carlos' one and only decent free kick.

The result was a spectacular effort that Danny Tickle would have been proud of. It was as high as it was handsome.

"I was only joking," I protested.

We continued to struggle playing more with hope than any real pattern. Carew put the Villa ahead, flicking in from what looked like an offside position. Dave rang me at halftime to have a moan.

"Even Andy Gray said it was off," Dave said.

Listen, if it's good enough for Gray then it's good enough for me. It was a close call but we aren't even getting those now.

Geo had a bit of a spat with Cousin on the way down the tunnel and was replaced with Barmby in the second half. Maybe the Brazilian was questioning the big mans effort and work rate and in return Cousin asked if the little guy would be signing for Hull FC anytime soon. It just adds to our problems at the moment and shows that the players must be taking the managers call for fighting spirit far too literally.

Brown threw on Manucho and went 4-4-2. We immediately looked better as we went in search of an equaliser. It made me wonder why we didn't start with the same formation. I also wondered if David Burns would get a second bite of the cherry and be able to ask Phil Brown the question.

Despite the pressure and the two corners near the end when Myhill went up to try and cause some confusion in the Villa defence, it was just too little to late. Time ran out and our manager's plan got the exact same return of earlier in the season. Refereeing decisions aside, we didn't offer enough to win the game. The first half of the season yielded 27 points and the second just 7 so far, that is all we need to know right there and I don't even have ProZone at my disposal.

The question is; are we going to go out meekly with our heads bowed or will we fight to our very last breath? I know which the fans would prefer.

Hull City 1 Stoke City 2
Saturday 9th May 2009

I haven't mentioned my mate Phil for a while. Luckily for me, we have both been too busy and our paths haven't crossed. I made a special effort to pop and see him though, to offer my sincere condolences over his sad loss. I refer of course to the manner in which his beloved Chelsea became the Dear Departed, as far as the Champions League was concerned.

After playing magnificently over two legs they finally succumbed to the away goals rule when Barcelona scored in the fourth minute of time added on. A cruel way to go made all the worse by the fact that the referee and linesmen were up to current Premier League standards. Welcome to our world Phil. Chelsea had a fair claim for numerous penalties which surely would have put the game beyond the Spaniards.

Anyone for a UEFA anti-English Conspiracy theory then?

In comparison the other semi-final was a no win situation for the Mandarins of European Football. I doubt if Monsieur Platini even bothered to tune in as the Red Devils destroyed the Gunners. I watched the game and I particularly enjoyed the mass Highbury exodus of loyal supporters as the third United goal went in with fully thirty minutes to go.

Now if I was Sir Alex I wouldn't risk any of my first eighteen players in what will probably be a completely meaningless last game of the season, especially as it comes just days before the Champions League final. Yes, rest the lot, that's what I'd do.

Getting back to Jeff Winter and his League of Extraordinary whatever, he has Stoke in the bottom three. It must be that as opposed to us, they have had the rub of poor refereeing decisions. It's not hard to understand why that would be the case though. That mob at the Britannia is enough to put the fear of God up anyone. Maybe if we could get anywhere near replicating their home crowd performance then we might get the important decisions to fall on our side of the line for a change. Ok so I'm clutching at straws at this late stage of the season but I'll take anything to give me hope right now. I even gave some credence to the latest mad cap conspiracy theory doing the rounds. Ask yourself this, if you were the manager of an inexperienced premier League side already looking ahead to your second season in the top flight, who would you want to stay up with you? Hull City, who are even more inexperienced or Newcastle with bags of experience and money to back it up? Yes I know I'm still clutching at those straws.

Phil Brown and Paul Duffen went to Chester races for some team bonding during the week. The idea was to try and relieve some of the pressure surrounding the team. Apparently the first team didn't go; they thought it was better to concentrate on the job in hand. I could do with something to take the strain away myself. I'm not joking, I have started to get a tightness across my chest at times of high stress, you know, pressures of work, telephone bills, Hull City matches, that type of thing.

As we drove to the ground I saw some stoke fans walking through the town. We pulled alongside them at a set of traffic lights and I couldn't resist the urge to have a word.

"Why?" I shouted to them.

"What?" One of the web toed wonders replied.

"Why?" I said again.

"Why what?"

"Why Delilah?"

The lights changed and I drove off before I could get the answer but glancing in my rear view mirror, I could see the Stoke fans shaking their six fingered fists as I went on my way.

More bad news came before kick off when a scan revealed that our captain had sustained knee ligament damage at Villa. Phil Brown tried to put a brave face on it saying that we'll know more when the doctors can do an exploratory operation but realistically Ash will join Gardner and Bullard in the sick bay and play no further part in the season.

Without Ian Ashbee, correction the Almighty Ian Ashbee, we generally look a poorer side. I still expected the lads to roll up their sleeves and give Stoke a game though. The club acted quite smartly in moving the advertising hoardings in from the sides of the pitch to within a yard of the touchline. The idea was to limit Delap's run up and resulting long throws. The tactic seemed to work a treat as old Rory was pretty much anonymous throughout the game. We looked fairly comfortable in the first half, had a couple of decent chances and certainly didn't play like a side under too much pressure. Almost against the run of play Fuller scored from a Stoke corner and for the umpteenth time this season we went into the break down by the odd goal. We toiled tirelessly in the second half but with the possible exception of Nicky Barmby the quality just isn't there in the final third.

Our spirit was broken completely when Liam Lawrence scored a spectacular long range goal that just about ended the game.

Andy Dawson restored a little bit of pride but little else when he grabbed the ball from Geovanni to claim a free kick and put it brilliantly past the grasping Sorenson in the Stoke goal. Once again the fight back came too late and I clutched my chest after yet another defeat. God knows what Phil Brown and the rest of the backroom staff are going through. I've got to learn to relax between matches or I may not make it to the end of the season. The Stoke hoards chanted relentlessly.

'Tango, Tango, what's the score,' must have been ringing in Phil Brown's ears all weekend. One of the daily newspapers had an article showing our manager as David Brent, with matching quotes. I hadn't realised that he had wound up so many people. The Stoke manager has performed minor miracles to ensure a second term in the top flight. I take my baseball cap off to Tony Pulis. Our own fans appeared totally deflated and many more than usual headed for exits early. It reminded me of the Arsenal crowd the other night. I wasn't laughing now and that's for sure. It feels as if the life is draining out of our season. Phil Brown isn't talking to Radio Humberside but did speak on TV that evening. Like the fans and the team he is beginning to look desperate. He said all the right things but not with any real conviction.

I hate to admit it but The fat lady is definitely gargling now.

Bolton Wanderers 1 Hull City 1
Saturday 16th May 2009

More stress came my way back at work. Not from the usual source this time but from another of my workmates.

Tony is very knowledgeable and almost always talks a lot of sense unlike Phil. He is a real 'glass is half empty' type of person sometimes though. Years of living in Hull can do that to you if you let it I suppose.

"Morning Tony," I said.

"That's it now," he said

"We can still do it Tony."

"Oh come on Pete, City are as good as down."

Talk about pessimistic. I have to believe that while it's still possible to do it, we can escape relegation. I know we have been sliding down in instalments and I know we show no sign of stopping the rot but I go into every game with hope and until that fat bird is on stage belting it out, then we are still a Premier League team.

Everybody was keeping an eye on the big north east derby. Phil Brown was at the game, he must be a sucker for punishment. I preferred to avoid it and check the score on Teletext later on. The result would have a massive impact on our season come what may. Obviously a draw would be the best for us but even a narrow Boro win wouldn't be the end of the world. Newcastle won 3-1, we swapped places with them and dropped into the bottom three for the first time this season and it certainly looked like things were going to be very difficult indeed.

It's also quite awkward for our honourable members of parliament at the moment. Almost everyday a fresh one is outed for some sort of abuse of their expenses system. It turns out that they are claiming for everything from wallpaper to repairs to toilet seats or quite ironically bags of manure. While they are not exactly breaking the rules there is no doubt that they are taking advantage. A lot of MP's are up to their necks in it and are rightly being exposed for their trouble.

For the last time this season we made the relatively short trip across to Lancashire. Apart from our visit to Blackburn way back in the second week of the season and the time when we had Liverpool on the ropes in December, our visits to the north west have mostly been fruitless. Having slipped into the bottom three for the first time our fate was no longer in our own hands and it meant that we would have to go for the win. Nigh on five thousand supporters travelled to get behind the team and be that much needed twelfth man. Our following has been nothing short of outstanding this season and no doubt part of the reason why we have done so well away from home. There was a good mix of fans at a local pub and the atmosphere was upbeat and jovial. Bolton were all but safe of course but our fans were happy to share a drink and a joke with them. It was a mixture of that end of season feeling and possibly the realisation that this could be very well be our last Premier League trip for a while.

The Reebok Stadium is an impressive sight. With four arched stands and inward sloping floodlights it almost looks like it's going to fall in on itself but it does give it a very modern feel. What a shame the club can't fill it.

There was a minutes silence before the game for a long standing servant to Bolton Wanderers who had passed away recently. It was a full minute and it was immaculately observed by both sets of fans. Thinking back to our home fixture on remembrance weekend when the Bolton fans couldn't keep quiet for thirty seconds, it was another indication of what great supporters we have.

Phil Brown went for an attacking line up with Barmby, Geovanni and Garcia supporting the front two of Manucho and Fagan. We played pretty well in the first half but still lacked that cutting edge in front of goal. Manucho spurned our best chance by rocketing over from about eight yards out. My granny....you know the rest.

We still had the majority of the game with Bolton seemingly happy to play for the draw. A promising attack broke down only for Bolton to go the full length of the field and lay the ball back for Steinsson to drive an angled shot past the partially unsighted Myhill.

Once again, we all got that sinking feeling. By halftime I was convinced we didn't have the firepower to come back.

We continued to play well in the second period and looked to get in to better positions in search of that elusive goal.

Fagan harried Danny Shittu, forcing him in to an error and then finished superbly with his left foot to level the scores.

Alice had met up with Peter Kay's brother at half time and was stood with him as the equaliser went in. They immediately went wild like everyone else and started jumping up and down as they hugged. Unfortunately their joint momentum started to take them down the gangway steps. They gradually increased speed like a runaway train. Neither of them had the sense to let go of the other as they careered relentlessly towards their doom. They ended up rolling to the bottom of the upper tier. Luckily they emerged without as much as a scratch, partly due to the fact that they collected other fans on the way down like toppling dominoes but mostly as the result of being under the influence.

City went on to dominate the second half but as with the home fixture a combination of great keeping from Jaaskelainen and a couple of extra coats of gloss on the woodwork kept us out.

News filtered through that Newcastle had been beaten at home by Fulham and had Bassong sent off. Middlesbrough had drawn with Villa at the Riverside and we were out of the bottom three again. The City fans lifted the roof off. We sang on and on for our team. Our fate was back in our own hands again. It was all set up for a cracking last day of the season. There could still be a few twists and turns but the simple fact was that if we matched Newcastle and Boro we would be a Premier League team next season. What a funny old game this really is.

West Brom's defeat to Liverpool meant the end for them. A real shame because they certainly tried to play the game the right way. Of the three teams that came up, everyone thought that the Baggies would be the best equipped to stay. It just didn't work out that way. Liverpool's victory wasn't enough to nick the title though. Manchester United won it again by virtue of a point against Arsenal at Old Trafford.

Love him or hate him, you have to admit that Alex Ferguson is an exceptional leader. With eleven League titles under his belt not to mention numerous FA cups, League Cups and the rest, he has to be the best manager anyone has seen in the modern game. Of course he has also won two European Champions League trophies and he is on for a hat trick this year.

That factor could be vital for us. I can't imagine that he would want to risk his stellar cast just days before the final against Barcelona. Manchester United's second team is still good enough to give anyone a game though and no one was counting their chickens just yet.

The tabloids were right on our case. In fact they were absolutely full of it. Let's be honest they are always full of it.

Back page headlines like, 'Who the Hull are they?' Questioned Ferguson's potential line up for the game against us. It did read like a 'who's that?' Rather than a 'who's who?' but until the big day it was all just media speculation. Other newspapers claimed that either Sunderland, Middlesbrough or Newcastle will launch legal proceedings against Manchester United if they field a weakened team and any of them end up going down as a result. Talking of full of it, Ian Wright gave a stunning example of his literary genius when he wrote in his newspaper column during the week. The Arsenal legend absolutely slated Phil Brown and hoped we were relegated rather than the team of his big mate Alan Shearer. I doubt if our manager lost any sleep over the remarks, especially as they come from a man who makes Coleen look like a Pulitzer Prize winner.

One of the quality newspapers avoided cheap headlines and had commissioned a think tank to come up with a Premier League table for managers. Ferguson was the stand out number one in the League but very surprisingly, Phil Brown was number four.

I know what you're thinking, with that awful second half to the season, how could he be the fourth best manager?

Let me give you a clue, Tony Pulis was third and it wasn't because of his sartorial elegance. Got it now, No?

Ok, I'll tell you. It was mainly down to money. If a manager outperforms the amount of cash his club spends then he will finish higher up the League, simple really.

Manchester United regularly shell out the equivalent of the gross domestic product of a small South American country. Hull City have spent next to nothing in comparison. The facts are clear. We had no right to expect the points total we amassed given the comparatively small amount of money that we'd spent on transfers and wages. It turns out that our boss has done a lot better than everyone thought.

Hull City 0 Manchester United 1
Sunday 24th May 2009

I noticed that Phil Brown's beard was back. It seems he's probably as superstitious as anyone else in Hull but if the Bolton performance was anything to go by, the tactic seemed to be working. It got me thinking. If I could recreate our build up to the play off final a year earlier then maybe we could get a similar outcome in this game. Ok, straw clutching on a grand scale I know but anything was worth a try. I even thought about booking into a local hotel the night before the game but all the ones we tried were full, so much for nobody wanting to come to Hull, eh? I went for a run on the morning of the game just like I'd done year earlier. I wore my lucky City socks and listened to my lucky songs on my lucky ipod. You know how I feel about coincidences but when I found out that the referee was Alan Wiley, the same man in the middle last year at Wembley, I was beginning to think that this could be our day. He would be in charge of two teams who sported the same colours as last year's finalists as well. All we needed was Dean Windass and we surely couldn't fail.

This was it now, the last game of the season, a year to the day since that wonderful Wembley match. To be fair having our fate in our own hands going in to this game was all we could hope for at the start of the campaign and now only the reigning League, European and World Champions stood in our way. From our lofty position at the halfway point of the season, it shouldn't have come down to this but it had, so we just had to knuckle down and get on with it.

I heard that some people were willing to sell their ticket for this game. I can't understand that. Probably the most important match in our history and some fans were considering selling out to the highest bidder. There was no way I would miss this, you'd have to prise the ticket away from my cold dead fingers.

I wore the same shirt I had worn at Wembley. I was leaving nothing to chance. We wanted to get to the ground early to try and soak up some of the atmosphere. Somehow, walking up Anlaby Road flyover didn't quite feel the same as Wembley Way, but it would do. As we got nearer to the ground there was definitely something in the air, a feeling that reminded me of our play off final. Scunthorpe had won a five goal thriller at Wembley by the odd goal earlier in the day. They would return to the Championship at the first time of asking. Good luck to them, maybe a little of their fortune would rub off on us and help cap an amazing weekend for the region.

Just like the game a year ago I didn't have any nerves, only it wasn't down to my faith in Phil Brown and his team this time. I just wasn't worried. I know people expect strange things to happen on the last day of the season but I just couldn't see any of the teams that could still go down getting a win. If that was the case then we would stay up and it wouldn't matter if Ferguson brought Steve Bruce, Gary Pallister and Eric Cantona back to play against us. No one would be able to complain.

I have to say that this was probably the best atmosphere I have ever witnessed at the KC stadium. The City fans fully got behind the team and gave it everything they had. The sizeable United support also got behind their side but I got the feeling that they weren't too fussy about this game. Their team was already the Champions and with a massive game on Wednesday, the fans probably had other things on their mind.

Alex Ferguson did put out a second string side in the end but it was still a Manchester United team. They really have to earn the shirt at that club and they certainly always go for the win. We started well and didn't seem to be suffering from nerves; in fact the young United stars looked the nervier.

It seemed strange to me that Phil Brown left our only two recognised centre forwards on the bench. We played tidy, decent football but yet again with no real cutting edge. News came through that Villa had taken the lead against Newcastle. The crowd gave the biggest cheer of the game and the United fans responded with a burst of 'Cheer up Alan Shearer,' which resonated around the ground.

The young United players never gave us too much trouble and I was convinced that we were heading for a goalless draw.

Darren Gibson found himself in far too much space on the left and unleashed a stunning right footed shot across Myhill's goal and into the net. We had been undone by that Premier League quality again. Our disappointment was short lived as the crowd went wild once more. Villa had the ball in the net again over in Birmingham. Unfortunately the goal was disallowed and our joy subsided.

Folan was brought on to replace Geovanni. If newspaper reports are to be believed, that might be the last we see of our talented Brazilian. He'll always be remembered for his skill and stunning goals, not the disappointing way his season has faded. We looked a lot brighter up front but still played without any real urgency. It was as if the players didn't realise that an equaliser at Villa Park would send us down. United played possession football to comfortably see out the game and just like all those years ago, we came second.

We had a nervous few moments while we waited for the other scores to come through but when they did, everyone went wild. Alex Ferguson allowed himself a wry smile and shook Phil Browns hand, they will get to meet again next season and the wily old Scot will probably put out a very different side.

In the end all four teams lost and that meant Newcastle and Boro had joined Albion on their way down to the Championship. Losing a game never felt so good. Only Gary and Tony missed out, they needed the draw to win their bets.

There was a pitch invasion of course. I don't think that anyone could begrudge the fans their few moments of joy. After everything we have been through this season it was just such a relief to finally be over the finishing line. The fans ran on and danced around and chanted and sang and when they eventually returned to the stands Phil Brown emerged with a microphone. He started to sing 'This is the best trip I've ever been on.' I remembered his performance on the balcony of the City Hall a year ago. I knew he had been drinking then but this time there surely was no such excuse. When I watched Match of the Day later in the evening Alan Hansen said he hoped that our manager would learn to be a bit more reserved next season.

Lineker said, "I don't know about that."

He's right. I can't see Phil Brown changing his style for anyone; he's too set in his ways for that. If he learns from his mistakes and improves our results from the second half of the season then most of the City fans will be happy though.

The players eventually came out on to the pitch for their obligatory lap of honour. No one left early, we all stayed to salute our 'heroes' as David Bowie's anthem blasted from the stadium speakers. As we watched them walk around the pitch, I couldn't help wondering who would be leaving and who would be staying for the next season.

We made our way across the car park just as the coaches carrying the Manchester United fans were starting to leave. We stood and applauded them and they responded by cheering and waving back at us. It reminded me of when we went to Cardiff and won the game which virtually sealed Leeds United's fate. This was one of those very rare occasions when both sets of football fans are happy, no matter what the score is. I'm sure that the United fans were especially pleased that Newcastle had been relegated seeing as Shearer had taken them there. They will not have forgotten that he spurned them and Alex Ferguson when he was in his prime as a player.

We'll be joined in the Premier League by Wolves and Birmingham next season. Burnley also managed to overcome

Sheffield United in the play off final. I can't wait to get in touch with the Blades fan in Portsmouth.

Milo rang me later that evening.

He was out with his mates celebrating. He said lots of things, some of which I could actually understand. Strangely he never mentioned the football match. As a game it was pretty forgettable but a Premier League season is about thirty eight games and not just the last one.

Over the course of those games we were good enough to stay in the division, just good enough.

"Pete, that was the best day of my life," he said.

"Milo, it was the best day of your life so far."

The Final Whistle

Our first ever season in the top flight ended almost as quickly as it began. Sadly it was much too brief. From the glorious start when we entertained Fulham, to our last game of the season against the Premier League Champions Manchester United, it was over in the blink of an eye.

As a newly promoted club, we got one of the most remarkable starts to a season that anyone had ever seen. By the end of December we had amassed 27 points by virtue of some stunning performances. No team had ever gone out of the Premier League with that kind of start. Wouldn't it have been just like us to set that particular record straight though? At the end of October we were joint top of the League and in December still a very respectable sixth. Then it started to go wrong. The decline saw us slide inexorably towards the relegation trap door but still we only entered the bottom three in May, with just two games remaining. At that stage there was still hope though. We went to Bolton and played exceptionally well. We should have won but the point we did get was enough to lift us back out of the bottom three. We went into the last game at home against Manchester United knowing that we had to match what Boro and Newcastle did to stay up. In the end that's exactly what we did do and in the end we sang and cheered and hugged friends and family and total strangers. Up in the north east the fans indulged in John Terry style histrionics. I felt sorry for them but I'm glad it was them and not us. Bill Shankly famously once said that football was more important than life and death. Of course it isn't, it just seems like it is sometimes.

There will be the usual end of season post mortem as we mull over what should have been and what would have been and what very nearly could have been, if....That bloody word if.

The simple truth is that relative inexperience at the top level nearly cost us dear. We got carried away with our phenomenal start. At one point I think Paul Duffen was talking about qualifying for Europe. Phil Brown may have started to believe his own press a little too much and one or two of the players got far too big for their own boots. It was all too easy to get carried away and even easier to forget that it's not where you start, it's where you finish that matters. Of course the fans who have seen us snatch defeat from the jaws of victory far too many times to mention, remained reasonably level headed. We will go through it all over again next season. How will we do? If we learn from our mistakes then we give ourselves a chance but nothing more than that.

Hull City football club doesn't have a distinguished past and our trophy cabinet contains precious little in the way of silverware but we came into the top flight of English football for the first time in our history this season and we gave it a real go. We won over many fans with our style of play and we genuinely brought much needed colour to an often monochrome League. No one can say that we didn't deserve to be in the top flight or that we don't deserve to have another crack at it next season.

As for our much maligned city. Staying up is hugely important, especially at a time of such economic depression. Relegation would have been a complete disaster. Over the course of the last year Hull has benefited greatly from being the home of a Premier League team. Retention of that status for the forthcoming year gives us an enormous boost in our bid to ride out the recession and to be ready to develop when the time comes. For those who aren't sure, Hull is already a very decent place and much better for knowing. Just ask the people who came to stay, or the people who left and wished they hadn't. Peter Taylor admitted that it was a big mistake to leave Hull, not just the team but the area as well. He allowed himself to be lured away when London was calling and it was something he will always regret.

Time will tell if the club and the city will go on to even greater things but before anyone bets against us, it's worth remembering that the future is unwritten. To that extent, it's still all to play for.

At the end of this season I felt compelled to stick two fingers up to all our detractors, to all those who said that our football team would do a 'Derby' and to all those who knock our city. Bjørge Lillelien famously lambasted all and sundry in 1981, after Norway humbled England 2-1 in a World Cup Qualifier. I think our achievements this season have eclipsed Norway's giant killing exploits, so with that in mind I will leave you with the following passage. When I had written it, I read it out loud in my best Norwegian accent. It gave me enormous pride and immense satisfaction; I hope you feel the same.

'To the Blade's fan in Portsmouth, who said we'd only last one season, to Mark Lawrenson, Alan Hansen, Andy Gray, Gary Lineker, Alan Shearer, Lee Dixon, Martin Keown, Bobby Robson, Terry Venables, Dan Kieran, Ian Abrahams, Mike Parry, Micky Quinn, David Mellor, Adrian Chiles, Chris Waddle, Kenny Dalglish and to every bookmaker and newspaper editor in the country....Your predictions took one hell of a beating.'